How the Cold War Is Taught

How The Cold War Is Taught

Six American History Textbooks Examined

Martin F. Herz

Ethics and Public Policy Center
Georgetown University
Washington, D.C.

Printed in the United States of America

Library of Congress Cataloging in Publication Data:

Herz, Martin Florian, 1917-
How the cold war is taught : six American history textbooks examined.

1. United States—Foreign relations—1945- —Study and teaching—United States. 2. World politics—1945- —Study and teaching—United States. 3. United States—Foreign relations—Russia—Study and teaching—United States. 4. Russia—Foreign relations—United States—Study and teaching—United States. 5. United States—History—Text-books. I. Title.
E744.H485 327.73 78-11053
ISBN 0-89633-009-5

CONTENTS

Introduction

Teaching History Backwards

The study of history, as Harry Truman was fond of pointing out, is the best schoolmaster for developing an understanding of public issues and for engendering a sense of civic responsibility. And certainly that slice of history one consciously lives through has the greatest impact on one's understanding and behavior.

The foreign-policy outlook of Americans in their forties and fifties has been fashioned by such dramatic events as Pearl Harbor, Hiroshima, the Berlin blockade, the Korean War, and the Cuban missile crisis. The younger generation's view of American responsibility abroad has been formed largely by the Vietnam War, the protest movement, and the domestic attacks on U.S. military and intelligence agencies so vividly mirrored in the American mass media.

Except for the few people who study the past seriously, neither generation is greatly influenced by events that unfolded a hundred or a thousand years ago. Yet most high school seniors probably know more about ancient Greece and Rome and the voyages of Columbus than about the recent events that have shaped the outlook of their parents. This disparity between what they know and what their parents know is one reason for the persistent generation gap. A reference to the Korean War will probably evoke a less vivid image among high school students than mention of the Civil War, and if one speaks of Senator McCarthy, they are likely to think of Gene rather than Joe.

The teaching of recent history is vital for any people. It is especially so for the United States, which is a democracy, a super-power, and the leader of the free world. The exercise of U.S. power and influence or the failure to exercise it has global reverberations. A responsible American citizen must understand this and must also be aware of the external dangers which threaten our freedom or that of our allies.

President Truman demonstrated such understanding and awareness when he responded to the North Korean attack on South Korea in 1950, comparing it to the unchallenged Japanese invasion of Manchuria two decades before, which eventually led to Pearl Harbor. "It was clear to me that Japan should have been stopped when it entered Manchuria in 1930," Mr. Truman later recalled, adding: "If Mussolini had been stopped from his conquest of Ethiopia, Hitler never would have had the guts to march on Poland" (*New York Times,* April 11, 1954).

Truman's decisions as President illustrate both a long-range sense of history and a recognition that we can learn from recent history. A sense of history—an appreciation of the forces that shape men and nations—is perhaps a gift, but it is surely enhanced by a disciplined knowledge of the past as well as by wisdom gained from religion, philosophy, psychology, and firsthand observation of the human drama.

The present high school generation, it can be fairly said, is only vaguely aware of the recent and current drama of world politics, except as it is communicated by perceptive parents or teachers or as it is portrayed on television. Consequently, the portion of American-history textbooks devoted to events that formed their parents' understanding of the larger world assumes special significance. This material, properly taught, helps to bring coherence and balance to episodic, fragmentary, and distorted snatches of recent history that the student may have picked up.

In terms of both understanding and responsibility, the immediate past bears the closest relation to the immediate future. Therefore, a case can be made for *teaching history backwards*. Perhaps the schools should start with the past thirty years, which provide the background for our most momentous current problems, and then move on to the more distant developments that formed these United States and Western culture. The past would then illuminate the present, and the present would pose questions for the future.

It is vitally important that high school textbooks portray the turbulent Cold War period fairly and intelligibly, with due regard to America's role in the international arena, and with a full recognition of the challenges presented by our chief adversary, the Soviet Union. The portrayal should include at least a brief explanation of the profound differences in political morality and behavior between American democracy—with its limited government—and the Soviet totalitarian system, noting some of the foreign-policy implications of a messianic state that seeks to bring secular salvation to peoples beyond its borders. How well is this being done by American-history textbooks?

This question is addressed in the present study. Its author, Ambassador Martin F. Herz, is a career Foreign Service officer and historian who is highly qualified to undertake this analysis of six widely used textbooks. Currently a Senior Research Fellow at the Ethics and Public Policy Center and Adjunct Professor of Diplomacy at the Edmund Walsh School of Foreign Service, both at Georgetown University, Mr. Herz has held diplomatic posts in Western Europe, Central Europe, Eastern Europe, the Middle East, and East Asia, and various other State Department positions, including Deputy Assistant Secretary for International Organization Affairs. He is also the author of *A Short History of Cambodia* (1958) and *Beginnings of the Cold War* (1969).

This study is the second in a textbook-analysis series being published by the Ethics and Public Policy Center. In this project, the Center seeks to assess how social-science textbooks present the core values of our American heritage and the internal problems of and external challenges to a free, pluralistic society. The Center affirms the moral validity and political relevance of the great Western ethical imperatives such as respect for the human person, individual freedom, justice, religious tolerance, the rule of law, limited government, and respect for private property. It affirms also that the United States, as a great and democratic society, has a moral obligation to use its power and influence for greater peace and security in the world.

The Center as such takes no position on specific domestic or foreign-policy issues. The authors of our publications, whether staff or consultants, speak only for themselves.

ERNEST W. LEFEVER, *Director*
Ethics and Public Policy Center

Washington, D.C.
October 1978

ONE

Scope, Method, Approach

The term *Cold War* became part of our vocabulary after the columnist-philosopher Walter Lippmann used it to describe the precarious state of "neither war nor peace" that prevailed between the Soviet Union and the Western democracies after World War II. Later the term was applied also to the interaction between the United States and the Chinese People's Republic and Cuba. Some historians believe that the Cold War can be dated from 1946, the year in which Winston Churchill remarked at Fulton, Missouri, that an "iron curtain" had descended between Soviet-occupied Eastern Europe and the democratic countries of Western Europe. The author of this analysis believes that the beginnings of the Cold War can be discerned earlier, in the controversies—then still secret—between Russia and the Western allies during the last phases of World War II in Europe.

Historians differ on whether the Cold War is still going on, or whether we have entered upon a period of no-war-no-peace that differs substantially from the immediate post-war period. All historians agree, however, that the Cold War is, or has been, a very important chapter in recent history and that its effects are still with us today. It is responsible for the large armed establishments of East and West, for the "balance of terror" that preserves (we must hope) a precarious peace, and for the way the peoples of East and West look upon the position of their countries in the world.

Why Knowledge Is Important

A good understanding of the Cold War is necessary if informed American citizens are to evaluate intelligently—to support or to challenge—the national-security and foreign policies of their government. Many of the facts about the past crises have sunk below the level of ready recall even for people who lived through them. Yet many of today's problems can be understood only in relation to what preceded them, for they are the legacy of earlier, unsolved problems.

As for our young people, how well or how poorly they are informed about this chapter of our history could affect the future options of our government in assuring the security of the United States and maintaining its values in a hostile world. It is therefore worthwhile to examine how the principal facts about the Cold War are conveyed to America's youth.

How Is the Cold War Taught?

The main sources of young people's knowledge about the recent history of the United States are their parents, television, and the high schools. Of these three, only the last is able to convey the story as a whole, in large outline. How well this is done depends to a considerable extent on the quality of the textbooks. The Cold War is a complex and controversial subject. The task of the teacher, and of the textbook writer, is not an easy one.

All the textbooks on American history now being used in the eleventh grade contain a chapter about the Cold War, usually taking the story right up to the time when the particular textbook (or its latest revision) went to press. Our study examines how that topic is taught and how well it is taught. We recognize that a high school textbook cannot be overly sophisticated, that it cannot possibly be comprehensive, and that special efforts must be made to hold the attention of young people, particularly those with limited reading ability.

Standards of Evaluation

There is no one "right" way of teaching the Cold War. Any chapter dealing with it will have a point of view; it is impossible to write history without one. Even if no opinions are expressed, the selection of facts, and the importance the author assigns to certain events and trends, reflect his intelligence and value system.

Recognizing the inevitability of a point of view, we still must measure the textbooks against certain standards. We are less concerned with comprehensiveness than with whether the textbooks convey a rounded picture of East-West relations since World War II. This involves judgments about accuracy and that elusive quality called fairness. We try to ascertain fairness in this manner: If a textbook expresses a strong opinion (either explicitly or in the way facts are chosen), we try to determine whether it also provides an opportunity for contrary opinion to be expressed. We ask also: Is the information it conveys accurate? Does it provide perspective, making the flow of developments understandable? Does it convey the view of its authors openly or surreptitiously?

One of the textbooks we analyzed, in an edition annotated for history teachers, carries a comment that exemplifies what we mean by "making the flow understandable." On the page that summarizes containment of Communism, the Truman Doctrine, the Berlin airlift, and the Marshall Plan, a note to the teacher says:

> Students should realize that this chapter supplies background for acute current problems. You know that they will forget details but the measure of your success will be, in part, the degree to which they retain interest in the problems so they will follow the developments on their own.

The flow of narrative must be not only interesting but also, where possible, internally consistent. Some events and developments become more understandable if their relation to previous events and developments is explained.

The Question of Bias

An accusation of bias must not be made lightly, and certainly not on the basis of only one or two instances. Nor should any interpretation, or even cluster of interpretations, be taken as lacking in "fairness" so long as differing interpretations are presented also. If, however, a book displays a consistent pattern of skewing the evidence or providing one-sided interpretations, it can be properly judged to be biased.

That the writers are aware of this problem is well illustrated by the following quotation from one of the textbooks:

> All people have opinions. An opinion is a belief a person holds which is biased on what seems to that person to be factually true. As you know, some opinions are very biased . . . . The person with a bias is prejudiced and narrow in the sense that he ignores viewpoints and facts that disagree with his bias. A strongly biased opinion is closed to new evidence and is therefore oversimplified . . . .

Bias is not a matter of accuracy. A book can contain accurate items of information but be so one-sided in its selection of them that it projects bias according to the definition presented above.

As proof of even-handedness, some authors point to the fact that their textbooks have been "criticized from the right and the left." This doesn't really seem an adequate test, for the criticisms from one side might be justified whereas the other side might only be complaining that the textbook didn't go still further in its preferred direction.

Two Teaching Approaches

Some books are mainly narrative, others consist largely of selected readings, and others are a combination of both. The so-called inquiry approach, which consists of presenting documentary information and encouraging the students to draw their own conclusions, appears to be used primarily with students who possess more highly developed reading skills and perhaps also higher intelligence than their peers.

We saw no reason why the same standards should not be applied to both the narrative and the "inquiry approach" books—whether they present facts accurately, treat the various facts and events fairly, and give an opportunity for contrary views to be heard. Even the books given over largely to readings contain introductions that summarize the particular event or episode of the Cold War about which various readings are then offered, and of course the selection of readings could be balanced or one-sided.

Choosing the Textbooks

We tried, first, to identify six of the most widely used textbooks for the eleventh grade. This was not easy. Publishing houses are reluctant to give out sales figures on textbooks—though the most successful publishers will gladly reveal that their textbooks are leading the pack, and their rivals will generally concede that they are somewhat behind the leaders.

After checking also with textbook authors, senior educators, and high school history teachers in different parts of the country, we are quite certain that the two top sellers are among the six textbooks we analyze and that the other four are widely used—though their sales figures fluctuate. Unless regularly revised, high school textbooks tend to decline in sales rather rapidly.

The annual market for eleventh-grade textbooks on American history is probably on the order of 750,000. One of the books we analyze, textbook A, has by general agreement probably sold more than 2.5 million copies since 1954, when it was first published. (For simplicity, since each book has more than one author, we identify them as A, B, C, D, E, and F. The full titles and the authors are listed further on in this chapter.) Another, B, probably sold 200,000 copies in 1977 alone. At least two of the others have at one time or another had a sales figure of more than 100,000 in a single year.

Two candidates for inclusion in our study had to be eliminated. One was so new that it had not yet established a track record. The other, once among the most widely used, had not been revised in nine years.

Method of Analysis

We have broken the subject down into sixteen sections. Each section is preceded by a short introduction entitled "Criteria." *The reader should bear in mind that these "Criteria" do not purport to prescribe how the subject should be treated. Nor do they represent summaries of the particular event.* The "Criteria" paragraphs merely call attention to some of the salient facts and point out problems of interpretation. They provide no more than a setting for our analysis of the textbooks, alerting the reader to aspects that a textbook writer might find difficult to handle.

Although textbooks must be selective in dealing with the Cold War because of the great number of relevant events, certain fundamental facts are essential to an understanding of post-war American foreign policy. For example, a student cannot understand the dispute between the Soviet Union and the West immediately after World War II without knowing about the wartime agreements of the Big Three allied powers, particularly those at Yalta in February 1945. Likewise, U.S. behavior is difficult to understand if the student is not acquainted with the policy of "containing" Soviet power.

Other developments are important but not central, and a conscientious author may choose to mention some and omit others. An American-history text need not, for example, analyze the internal political system of the Soviet Union. (Several do, however, and so we compared their treatments of that subject.) Likewise, a textbook of American history need not treat Soviet military intervention in Hungary in 1956 or in Czechoslovakia in 1968. But if it carried no information about the establishment of Soviet satellite regimes in Eastern and Central Europe between 1944 and 1948, or about Soviet territorial claims on Turkey, or about the Soviet breach of the agreement to withdraw from Iran in 1946, there would be reason to be concerned about its fairness and balance.

The Topics

Most of the sixteen topics we examined are on our list by virtue of their importance, but some—for instance, topic 3—were included only because of the attention given them in several of the texts. Despite its imperfections, this list provides a rough framework for a systematic assessment of the scope, accuracy, and balance of the textbook treatment of the Cold War:

1. Origin and Meaning of the Cold War
2. Communism, and the Nature and Aims of the Soviet Union
3. How the Russians May Have Viewed the West
4. The Yalta Agreements and Their Aftermath
5. The U.S. Policy of Containment
6. The Truman Doctrine
7. The Berlin Blockade (1948–49) and the Berlin Wall (1961)
8. The United Nations and the Cold War
9. The Korean War (1950–53)
10. McCarthy and Anti-Communism in the 1950s
11. Castro's Rise to Power
12. The Bay of Pigs (1961) and the Cuban Missile Crisis (1962)
13. Early U.S. Involvement in Vietnam
14. The Tonkin Gulf Resolution (1964)
15. Late Vietnam Developments
16. Has the Cold War Ended?

This is not to say that all these subjects must be treated in a textbook of this kind. Nor do we claim that the list is complete; it does not include, for instance, the Marshall Plan, NATO, the Cominform, or the civil war in China. Furthermore, we are not suggesting that any of the topics has to be treated in a particular way. Historians may argue where the "truth" lies in history; but they don't argue whether North Korea invaded South Korea in 1950 or whether it was the other way around (as the Soviet Union argued, rather lamely, for a while), nor do they disagree about whether that event had important effects on how the East was perceived by the West. Whether the American reaction to the invasion of South Korea was wise, whether our response was carried too far—these are matters of judgment; but it is difficult to see how the Cold War can be adequately presented without some reference to the unprovoked aggression of Communist North Korea against its neighbor to the south.

The Six Textbooks

A. *History of a Free People*, by Henry W. Bragdon, Samuel P. McCutchen, and Charles W. Cole. New York: Macmillan Publishing Company. Copyright 1973. Earlier editions copyright 1954, 1956, 1958, 1961, copyright 1964, 1967, 1969.

B. *Rise of the American Nation*, by Lewis Paul Todd and Merle Curti. New York: Harcourt, Brace Jovanovich. Copyright 1977, 1972, 1969, 1966, 1964, 1961, copyright 1950.

C. *The American Experience*, by Robert F. Madgic, Stanley S. Seaberg, Fred H. Stopsky, and Robin W. Winks. Menlo Park, Calif.: Addison-Wesley Publishing Company. Copyright 1975.

D. *A New History of the United States—An Inquiry Approach*, by Irving Bartlett, Edwin Fenton, David Fowler, and Seymour Mandelbaum. New York: Holt, Rinehart and Winston. Copyright 1975, 1969.

E. *The People Make a Nation*, by Martin W. Sandler, Edwin C. Rozwenc, and Edward C. Martin. Boston: Allyn and Bacon. Copyright 1975.

F. *Discovering American History*, by Allen O. Kownslar and Donald B. Frizzle. New York: Holt, Rinehart and Winston. Copyright 1974, 1970, 1967.

A, B, and C are essentially narrative, and D, E, and F are mixtures of narrative and readings, E consisting largely of readings.

How Textbooks Are Adopted

The textbook business is controlled by the marketplace, but that marketplace is a complicated one in which the choice is limited. A new textbook must pass through a number of stages. The initial writing is usually done by several authors. Then there are likely to be extensive revisions by the publisher, who is sensitive to the currents and cross-currents of the educational community and of the market. The text may have to be expanded or abbreviated to accord with graphic materials, such as charts and illustrations. A newly published textbook may be distributed on an experimental basis and then further revised to eliminate material that might be objectionable to various interest groups.

After this it may be approved by state textbook-adoption committees (in states like California and Texas) or by local school boards.

Such approval doesn't necessarily mean that the book will be bought, however, for usually it is only placed on a list from which the schools may choose. To get on the list, a textbook must meet certain prescribed norms; for instance, some approving authorities recently decreed that history textbooks must cover developments in America in the status of women and ethnic minorities and the rising concern over problems of the environment. As far as we know, there are no particular requirements regarding coverage of the Cold War.

Our study should be of interest not only to textbook authors, publishers, and teachers but also to students and parents—and to other readers who are concerned about problems of public policy.

Two

The Six Textbooks Examined

This chapter makes up the body of our study, a comparative analysis of how the six history books present sixteen salient foreign-policy events or issues to their readers. Each topic is introduced by a brief statement—"Criteria"—setting forth the chief points and possible difficulties; this is followed by an analysis of the treatment given the topic in each of the textbooks. It should be reemphasized that the "Criteria" do not purport to be summaries, nor do they attempt to prescribe how a given subject must be treated. Also, it is not necessary for all topics to be covered. Hence the analysis is presented in narrative and nonquantitative form.

1
Origin and Meaning of the Cold War

Criteria

How did it happen that the United States and the Soviet Union, comrades-in-arms during World War II, found themselves in open disagreement on a number of issues almost immediately after the end of the war in Europe? Those disagreements arose in large part from the consolidation of Soviet power in the occupied parts of Eastern Europe. The United States and Great Britain took the position that Soviet actions in Eastern Europe contravened the agreements concluded in February 1945 at Yalta.

The source of the greatest disagreement was the Polish issue. How Poland was to be governed had been discussed by the U.S.S.R., Great Britain, and the United States on many occasions during the war. An agreement signed at Yalta called for reorganization of the Polish provisional (Communist) government and for free elections. There was also a declaration that seemed to require the Soviet Union to facilitate democratic elections in other Eastern European countries.

One can believe that Yalta represented a "sellout" to the Russians, or that the Yalta agreements were reasonable but the Soviets broke them, or that the agreements lent themselves to differing interpretations, or that the West had no business concerning itself with the Communist takeovers in Eastern Europe; but the fact should not go unmentioned that those takeovers, and the ensuing purges of non-Communists, caused rising concern in the West, where the Soviet Union seemed like a new aggressor.

Immediately after the war, the Soviet Union also failed to honor its commitment to withdraw its occupation troops from northern Iran. It made territorial demands on Turkey, which had been neutral during the war. And it laid claims to very large reparations from Germany. But reparations from the western part of that country would in effect have been paid by the United States since the Germans were not able to pay for the American relief they were receiving. Such facts are relevant, and at least some of them should be mentioned.

Treatment

How is this difficult skein of events and developments presented by the various textbooks?

Textbook A* says: "*The quarrel was not of our choosing. On the contrary, Americans wanted to get along with Russia. . . . It became increasingly clear, however, that it was no more possible to appease Stalin than Hitler. Russian actions changed American good will to fear and distrust. By 1946 Stalin had apparently decided that no peace was possible between the capitalist and Communist worlds. Not only did he say so publicly, but his actions destroyed the big power unity which Roosevelt had tried to forge during World War II. In the countries of Central Europe that Russian armies had liberated from the Germans, the Communists established one-party governments which took orders from Moscow. All opposition, dissent, or free expression of opinion was ruthlessly suppressed.*"

There are minor factual errors in this treatment—most of the countries dominated by the U.S.S.R. after World War II are in Eastern, not

---

*Italicized passages are exclusively quotations from the authors of the textbooks. Wherever quotations are from selected readings in the textbooks, they are not italicized. The textbooks are identified on page 11.

Central, Europe, and most were in fact conquered rather than "liberated"—but the overall impression is that the authors of textbook A think there is no doubt who started the Cold War: it was the Soviet Union.

For comparison, let us look at a capsule formulation in textbook F: "*Gradually the Soviet Union and the other allies abandoned their wartime policy of mutual support and friendly relations. Hostile actions took place on both sides. And suspicions grew. Before long, an invisible boundary was set up between eastern and western Europe. The boundary was known as the 'iron curtain.' It divided Europe into two hostile groups. The western group of European countries favored and supported the policies of the United States. The eastern group favored the policies of the Soviet Union. Historians say that this division of East and West marked the beginning of the 'Cold War.' Historians do not agree on who started the Cold War.*"

Textbook F is non-committal. Things just happened. Nobody is responsible. The Iron Curtain was "set up" by no one in particular. The Eastern European countries "favored" the U.S.S.R.—they were not taken over by force and governed by Communist minorities controlled by the Soviet Union. The fact that some historians blame the United States for starting the Cold War leads the authors to throw up their hands and say, in effect, that it is not for them to say how and why things happened—although in other parts of the book they do assess blame against many aspects of American society and American policy.

Textbook B says that "*America's new role of world leadership brought it into conflict with the Soviet Union*," and it characterizes the policies of the U.S.S.R. as "*at least in part, a continuation of the expansionist ambitions of tsarist Russia*." It then refers to the incorporation of Latvia, Lithuania, and Estonia into the Soviet Union in 1940 (partially justifying it by saying that these were countries "*to which the Russians had some historical claims*," presumably because they had once been part of the tsarist empire) and reports that "*as a result of World War II, the U.S.S.R. also acquired large parts of Poland and Rumania. Through Communist governments which they helped to set up, the Soviets by 1948 had gained control of the 'free' governments of Poland, Rumania, Hungary, Czechoslovakia, and the Eastern part of Germany*." (For some reason, Bulgaria is not mentioned.)

Without going into details about what happened in Eastern Europe, textbook B makes it clear that the presence of substantial Soviet forces in that area, and the political changes that they helped to bring about, were perceived as a threat by the West: "*The United States, which had demobilized most of its own troops, resented the Soviet policy of maintaining huge forces. Moreover, Americans loathed the ruthless methods used by the Communists to crush all opposition. Most Americans regarded the Soviet Union as the world's newest aggressor.*"

Textbook C sees the Cold War as essentially a power struggle. The question of responsibility is not raised. The key passage on this subject reads: "*Both the United States and the Soviet Union employed almost every conceivable means from massive economic and military aid to psychological warfare to maintain their own positions of strength and to compete for the support of other nations. Although this kind of rivalry is not new to international politics, never before was it so intense and so fraught with danger for all mankind.*" The use of the word "rivalry" epitomizes the neutral stance of the book.

Textbook D, which relies to some extent on readings, has an introduction that first refers to the United Nations and then states: "*The world soon recognized, however, that the United States and the Soviet Union would not easily settle their differences over the conference table. The Soviet Union wanted a postwar world which would protect its boundaries and favor the expansion of Communism. The United States sought a democratic world in which American interests would be secure. The rivalry between these two nations became so intense that people began to refer to it as the 'Cold War.'*" Again, "rivalry" suggests a jockeying for position rather than a situation in which one side is trying to expand its power while the other is trying to contain it.

Textbook E, which consists mainly of readings, has only a cursory introduction to the subject. It reports: "*By the final years of the war, many people were becoming very suspicious of the aims of our ally the Soviet Union in the belief that the Soviet Union would use the conquest of Germany and the confused state of affairs in postwar Europe to further its own ambitions for new territory and power.*" It then says that "*between the years 1945 and 1948 the Soviet Union imposed Communist regimes on Albania, Bulgaria, Czechoslovakia, Hungary, Rumania, and Poland. Time and again the United States protested these activities to the Russian leaders. Gradually the two wartime allies . . . drew apart. Then a 'Cold War' began.*"

The selected readings provided by textbooks D, E, and F do not deal with the origin and nature of the Cold War. They will be discussed in connection with the policy of containment and the Truman Doctrine.

2
Communism, and the Nature and Aims of the Soviet Union

Criteria

Whether one sees Communism as a socioeconomic system, an ideology, or a form of government—or as all three—certain essential features should not be overlooked. Communism is revolutionary, defines all conflict as essentially motivated by class interests, and in practice denies civil and political rights as we know them to the people it controls. It is egalitarian in theory, though not in practice. Wherever it has come to power it has dealt very harshly with its opponents. Yet it has a powerful doctrinal attraction, especially where Communist parties are not in power, because it preaches a philosophy that purports to explain the past, the present, and the future, calls for the elimination of economic inequality and injustice, and promises its adherents that Communism's victory is historically inevitable.

Treatment

Textbook F says: "*Communism is a word used to describe a system of social organization based on common property, or an equal distribution of wealth. For example, in societies organized on communist principles all property would be owned by all the people in common. And each person would have an equal share of the wealth produced by society. No one member of the society would be able to become much wealthier than another.*"

Nothing here about any loss or deprivation of civil or political rights on the part of those who live under the Communist system, nothing about the brutalities of Communism in practice—but we are still dealing in history and theory. "*Lenin and his fellow revolutionaries,*" says textbook F, "*followed most of the principles of Karl Marx. They wanted to change Russian society so that the means of producing goods and services would be owned by all Russians in common. Private ownership of the means of production would be abolished. Everyone—not just certain groups—would share in the wealth produced by the nation.*" This is an attractive dream, and it is quite generous of the authors to spell it out in such detail before describing how it was applied in practice.

"*Because Russia was so backward,*" continues textbook F, "*Lenin believed that this type of society would take time to set up. At first, only a small group of revolutionaries would be capable of taking part in government. This group would be drawn from members of the Communist Party. They would direct Russian society on its new course. Later, when Russia had advanced, control would be given to the whole people.*" The intentions of Lenin and his colleagues, in other words, were pure. Not a word here about the severities they visited upon their opponents, the terror tactics of their secret police, and the dreadful sufferings inflicted upon the peasantry. However, we are still only with Lenin. His successor is treated as follows:

"*Under Stalin's rule, the Soviet Union took great strides forward. It grew from a backward agricultural nation into a giant industrial state. Natural resources were developed successfully. Large-scale heavy industry was built up. Individual farms were combined to form huge government-owned farms where more efficient farming methods were introduced. Illiteracy was fought throughout the nation. And programs were set up to re-educate the Soviet citizen.*"

Programs to "re-educate the Soviet citizen"? This may bring faint echoes of concentration camps, of the Gulag Archipelago—but the reader will find little about such matters. Nothing about the killing of millions of "kulaks" in the course of collectivization. Nothing about the purge trials, the increasing paranoia of Russia's ruler, the liquidation of an entire generation of revolutionaries. (It is perhaps no accident that, likewise, in the chapter on World War II textbook F makes no mention of the Stalin-Hitler pact of 1939.) However, not everything was perfect in the Soviet paradise—at least, not yet—for, this treatment of Communism continues:

"*Unfortunately, these improvements did not touch all parts of the Soviet life. The Russian people still did not have the power of self-government. The power remained in the hands of a small group of Communist party members. They continued to direct most aspects of Soviet life and to decide what was good or bad for the people. No opposition to their ideas was allowed. Anyone who dared to disagree with their methods of governing the Soviet Union was suppressed.*"

What is missing is any indication that dictatorship is of the essence of the Communist system. On the contrary, it is said that the Russian people "still" did not have the power of self-government, as if this would eventually flow from the beneficent nature of the system. No mention that Lenin and Stalin were dictators, that hundreds of thousands of innocent people were carted off to jail and even made to confess to crimes they hadn't committed. The system is pictured as essentially attractive, though "unfortunately" marred by certain minor blemishes.

This is then followed by the amazing statement that the Communists in the rest of Europe were—presumably before World War II—"*for the most part just one more minor political party in a country.*" It would not have been regarded as fair, one supposes, for textbook F to point to the role of the Communists in keeping the West disarmed in the face of Hitler, or indeed to their role in bringing him to power—since the motto of the German Communists had been that it would be better to have Hitler in power than the German Socialists. (Their slogan was "*Lieber Hitler als Hilferding!*"—rather Hitler than the Socialist candidate.)

So the pupil exposed to textbook F is likely to form a generally favorable view of Communism and to see Lenin and Stalin as basically well-intentioned leaders who, because of circumstances, were not yet able to bring complete freedom to the people they governed. Considering that most of the textbooks treat at length the shortcomings of the United States in areas of social, economic, and political justice over the centuries, one can only marvel at the benefit of the doubt accorded to the Soviet system in textbook F.

Textbook A presents a very different view of Communism. It doesn't go into the movement's early history but tries to analyze its ideological power: "*In the long run the Communists are probably more dangerous opponents than were the Fascists because the Communists' message has wider appeal. Most of the world lives in desperate poverty, and many millions are unemployed—the Communists promise work and a decent living for all. Millions suffer discrimination because of race or religion—the Communists declare that all men (at least all who work with their hands) are brothers. Many people, especially the young, want to find identity by dedicating themselves to a cause—the Communists call on all men and women of good will to join in a crusade against poverty and oppression. The Communists profess belief in government by the people and call the states they control 'people's democracies.' Often it is only after they have taken over a country that its people learn that the bright promises of communism are false and that they mask a totalitarian system of tyranny over body and mind.*"

Textbooks B, C, D, and E have nothing to say about this subject and should not be faulted on that score so long as they deal adequately with Soviet foreign policies that impinge on U.S. interests. Khrushchev's January 6, 1961, speech calling for "wars of national liberation," for example, would be a relevant historical fact in connection with the history of the years that followed.

However, two of the textbooks that say nothing about the nature of Communism (C and D) and one that does cover the subject (B) have something to say about how the Russians may have seen their own position vis-à-vis the West after World War II.

3
How the Russians May Have Viewed the West

Criteria

A "revisionist" school of historians considers that more blame for the outbreak of the Cold War attaches to the actions of the United States than to those of the Soviet Union. One can agree or disagree with this view, but in each case the question revolves around facts—intentions are very difficult to document. Revisionists have been accused of employing a double standard: they justify Russia's actions on the grounds of national security or historical experience but do not apply the same standards to the actions of the West, holding it, rather, to higher standards.

Where a textbook gives reasons why the Russians might have been justified in feeling or acting a certain way, it would not be unreasonable to expect also an explanation for why the Americans felt or acted the way they did. In other words, it may be commendable to try to see how the Cold War might look from the side of the Soviet Union, but this attempt should in fairness be accompanied by a similar look at the Western perspective, using the same criteria.

Treatment

Textbook B, after detailing the takeovers of governments in Eastern Europe, says: "*The Communist* [*Russian*] *leaders defended their ac-*

tions on grounds of self-defense. They pointed out that during the Bolshevik Revolution the Allies, including the United States, had sent troops into northern Russia and Russian Siberia. They feared, they said, that the United States would lead the 'capitalist nations' in a new attack against the U.S.S.R. They claimed that, to defend themselves against such an attack, they were required to maintain powerful military forces and to control bordering countries from which an attack might be launched." This is an interesting argument, but it overlooks the hypocrisy by which the U.S.S.R. in fact denies that it controls bordering countries. It is true that Stalin at Yalta argued that a "friendly Poland" and the cession of Polish lands east of the Curzon Line were essential to Soviet security, but the Soviet line is that the Red Army is in the Eastern countries by the freely expressed desire of their governments and populations, to protect them against "imperialist aggression," not for the benefit of the Soviet Union's security.

Textbook B also explains how the events in Eastern Europe looked from the American perspective, as we saw in section 1.

Textbook C devotes half a page to an explanation of the Russian perspective on the Cold War: The Western leaders, it says, "*underestimated the Soviet Union's traditional fear of the West. Only later did they realize collaboration to crush Hitler's Third Reich did not erase from Russian minds the memories of western intervention following the Bolshevik Revolution. Nor did collaboration soften the Russians' bitterness over the West's rejection of Soviet efforts to build an alliance against Hitler in the mid-1930's; or over British and French efforts, as exemplified in the Munich Pact, to turn the Nazi threat away from Western Europe toward the Soviet Union. . . .*"

"*American officials also erred,*" says textbook C, "*in evaluating Soviet thinking on key wartime decisions. They showed little, if any, understanding of how Stalin would interpret the delay in opening the second front in political rather than military terms; that he would consider it a deliberate attempt by the western powers to have Germany and the Soviet Union exhaust each other in conflict. Soviet fear of hostile western intentions was real, and it constantly undermined the chances for genuine friendship. The Soviet drive to dominate Eastern Europe in the postwar period can in part be attributed to this fear and the need for self-protection.*"

It would be easier to applaud this fair-minded presentation of the Soviet point of view if textbook C also contained the other side of those arguments and if it described what the U.S.S.R. and the people it put into power did to non-Communists in the Eastern European countries that it came to dominate. Instead, we find an apology for Soviet violations of human rights in purely power-political terms: "[*The*] *collapse of Europe's prewar power structure had opened Eastern Europe to communism. The Soviets saw little reason to make agreements which would allow capitalist powers again to gain power along their borders.*" This easy equation of democracy with "capitalism" may be a bit jarring to readers who look at such issues also in terms of fundamental human rights; and there is nothing about the threat to West European security as it might have been perceived through Western eyes at that time.

On the other hand textbook C is the only one that summarizes the post-World War II revisionist position—that most of the blame for the Cold War rests on the United States—and gives a reasoned rebuttal of that position. "*In recent years,*" says textbook C, "*some historians studying the origins of the Cold War have suggested it grew out of causes more complex than Communist expansion and western efforts to contain it. They hold that the Soviet actions in the immediate postwar period can best be understood as defensive behavior. They see the communization of Eastern Europe as a Russian attempt to protect the Soviet Union from Germany, which had already invaded Russia twice in the twentieth century. Rather than recognize that fear, the United States rearmed West Germany, increasing Soviet suspicions. These revisionist historians also view containment in Asia as serving more to identify the United States with corrupt, unrepresentative regimes than to provide the Asian people with positive alternatives to communism.*"

And in answer to that position, textbook C says: "*Other historians, however, reject the theory that the United States was equally responsible for the Cold War. They credit the Truman administration with both wisdom and foresight in meeting Soviet expansionism in Europe with programs like the Marshall Plan and the creation of NATO. They also suggest that Truman, Eisenhower, and Kennedy showed great restraint in crises such as Berlin, Korea, the Middle East, and Cuba, meeting Communist challenges while avoiding provocative actions that might have precipitated a third world war.*"

There is a certain imbalance in textbook C's treatment of perceptions. The revisionists are given a chance (actually two chances) to make their case about Russian perceptions of the West as a threat and about American immorality; but no one is given a chance to cite in rebuttal some facts about American perceptions of a Soviet threat and about Russian immoral behavior. Textbook C asserts only that the defensive *tactics* of the United States were moderate and non-inflammatory—not that U.S. policies or strategies or tactics were justified. (An argument crying out to be made, for instance, is that the rearmament of West Germany was a result, not a cause, of Russian expansionist actions in Europe after World War II. To a degree, it was also a reaction to Communist aggression in Korea.)

Textbook D is not particularly even-handed. How it treats Soviet objectives has already been noted in the first section ("*The Soviet Union wanted a postwar world which would protect its boundaries and favor the expansion of communism. . . . The rivalry* [*between the superpowers*] *became so intense that people began to refer to it as the 'Cold War'* "). It does describe American policies as "*designed to check the expansion of Communist influence*," but then remarks only that "*thousands of Americans died on distant battlefields in 'limited wars' defending those policies*." The Russians, in other words, defended interests and ideals; the Americans, "policies."

Textbook E, as we have seen in the first section, does mention the imposition of Communist regimes in Eastern Europe, but it does not interpret this as a cause of the Cold War.

Textbook F (which, as we shall see further below, alleges that President Truman called for intervention against "democratic revolutions . . . anywhere"), has nothing about how the suppression of democratic liberties in Eastern Europe, with police terror, show trials, and executions, might have looked from the perspective of Western Europe and the United States; neither, however, does it describe the Soviet perspective.

So far we have not mentioned textbook A in this section. This is because it does not describe the Soviet perspective. It seems to have no doubt that Russian actions were responsible for the outbreak of the Cold War. In fact, it contains a quotation that is unabashedly pro-American in describing U.S. programs and attitudes in the Cold War. The statement, attributed to a "group of scholars from Oxford University" in 1952, reads as follows:

"The faults and shortcomings of America—which, unlike those of the Soviet Union, are wide open to the world and freely discussed by the Americans themselves—have led too many people. . . to ignore the plain fact that the U.S.A. has been the best 'top nation' since Rome. It establishes order, resists the aggressor, defends the attacked, strengthens the weak, and succors the poor. The U.S.A. is the first world power to give money away, to tax itself for the foreigner in peacetime. We are too little astonished at the unprecedented virtuousness of U.S. foreign policy and at its good sense." It must be said that in this one instance textbook A goes further in showering roses on the United States than other textbooks go in exculpating the Soviet Union.

4

The Yalta Agreements and Their Aftermath

Criteria

The agreements concluded at Yalta in February 1945 fall into five broad categories: (1) On Poland, the U.S., U.S.S.R., and Great Britain agreed that the (Communist) provisional government would be "reorganized on a broader democratic basis with the inclusion of democratic leaders from Poland itself and from abroad" and that free elections would be held "as soon as possible." (2) A Declaration on Liberated Europe pledged the three signatories "to [restore] sovereign rights and self-government to those peoples who have been forcibly deprived of them by the aggressor nations" and that to this end the three powers would "jointly assist the people of any European liberated state or former Axis satellite . . . to form broadly representative [interim governments]" that would be pledged to the holding of free elections. (3) Reparations from Germany were set at a ball-park figure of $20 billion "as a basis for discussion." (4) Substantial agreement was reached on organization of the United Nations. (5) The U.S.S.R. exacted certain territorial and other concessions in the Far East in return for its pledge to join the other Allies in the war against Japan three months after the end of the war in Europe.

It would probably be asking too much to have all these agreements described and explained. Moreover, presenting the agreements in a simple manner is very difficult, because most of them had ambiguous elements. The agreement on Poland, for instance, could be interpreted (as it was by the West) as calling for a completely new government or (as it was by the U.S.S.R.) as calling only for some adjustments in the Communist-dominated provisional government. Similar ambiguities existed in the Declaration on Liberated Europe. High school textbooks could hardly be expected to go into an exegesis of these agreements. It is a fact, however, that there were no free elections in any of the countries occupied by the Russians (with the exception of Hungary in 1945 and the Russian zone of Austria). It is also a fact that the Russians were very dissatisfied when, at the Potsdam Conference later in 1945, the Western Allies refused them any substantial reparations from the western part of Germany. It is also relevant, though not essential to know, that the agreements on the Far East were later criticized because they had been made behind the back of the Chinese and because the Western concessions turned out to have been unnecessary when the atomic bomb helped to bring the war against Japan to an early conclusion.

Treatment

Four of the six textbooks give thumbnail summaries of the Yalta agreements. Where there are comments, they are by way of rebuttal of conservative criticism of those agreements. A good example of the treatment, one that parallels that of some other authors, is found in textbook B. This textbook first reports that critics of the Yalta agreement called it a "surrender" that resulted in Soviet control over Eastern Europe "without the free elections which Stalin had promised" and in Russian occupation of East Germany and East Berlin as well as of Manchuria and certain Japanese islands. It even mentions that some critics say that Yalta paved the way for the Communist victory in China and opened the door to Communist aggression in Korea. Textbook B then continues:

"Roosevelt's defenders have replied to these charges by reminding the critics of the military situation at the time of the Yalta Conference. Soviet armies had already conquered most of Eastern Europe, including Poland. American troops, on the other hand, had not yet crossed the Rhine and were still fighting the Japanese in the Philippines. Moreover, Allied military leaders had warned that the invasion of Japan, scheduled for the spring of 1946, would be extremely costly, and that the United States should be prepared to lose as many as 1 million troops.

"Perhaps most important, Roosevelt's defenders insisted, was the fact that Stalin had given Churchill and Roosevelt reason to believe that

the Soviet Union would cooperate in building a world organization designed to establish the foundations of a lasting peace. As Churchill himself later wrote, 'Our hopeful assumptions were soon falsified. Still, they were the only possible ones at the time.' "

Note that textbook B does not take a position of its own on the merits of the issues. It cites the attack, then the defense. Not so textbook A, which comes out with its own interpretation of the charges against the Yalta agreements:

"*The Yalta agreements later came under violent attack as a 'sell-out' to Russia. This charge ignored several facts. In the first place, it seemed vital to keep Russia in the war against Germany at a time when American forces had hardly recovered from the Battle of the Bulge and, even more important, to bring Russia into the war against Japan. It was expected that the defeat of Japan would cost from half a million to a million American lives and would take eighteen months. Secondly, no territorial concession was made to Stalin that the United States and Britain were in a position to prevent, except the Kurile Islands. Thirdly, Stalin on his part made concessions. The main trouble with Yalta was not the agreements themselves, but that Russia later broke them. . . .*"

What, then, are the things that Stalin failed to do? Here the texts are not equally specific. Textbook A refers to the Communists' establishing "*one-party governments, suppressing dissent and any free expression of opinion.*"

Textbook B makes the point by indirection: "*. . . Americans loathed the ruthless methods used by the Communists to crush all opposition. Most Americans regarded the Soviet Union as the world's newest aggressor.*"

Textbook C speaks only of "East-West rivalry" that "surfaced" after World War II. However, in connection with the Potsdam Conference it says: "*The Red Army's establishment of pro-Communist governments in Rumania, Bulgaria, and Hungary, in violation of the pledge to permit the liberated peoples of Eastern Europe to elect governments of their own choosing, and Stalin's refusal to permit free elections in Poland, created serious strains.*" The reference to Hungary is erroneous. There were free elections in that country in 1945. The Communist takeover came later.

Textbook D speaks of the Soviets' "installing" Communist governments in Eastern Europe.

Textbook E, which has nothing about Yalta, does mention the imposition of Communist regimes in Eastern and Central Europe, but it does not bring out that the American government thought this a violation of international agreements. (We shall see, in fact, in section 6 below, that textbook E "censored" President Truman by deleting his reference to violations of the Yalta agreements.) No sense is conveyed of any causal connection between the imposition of Communist regimes and the beginning of the Cold War, except perhaps by a remote and tenuous implication.

Textbook F, which we recall for its positive passages about the attractive features and good intentions of Communism, has nothing at all about the takeovers in Eastern Europe, nor does it report anything about Allied disagreements over Yalta, or about Russian actions in Iran and with respect to Turkey and Greece after World War II.

5
The U.S. Policy of Containment

Criteria

Although it was expressed in rather sophisticated terms by George F. Kennan in his article (signed "X") in *Foreign Affairs* in 1947, the essentials of the policy he recommended are found in the words "a firm policy of containment, designed to confront the Russians with unalterable counterforce at every point where they show signs of encroaching upon the interests of a peaceful world." In other words, the policy was designed not to expand the area of the West but to prevent any further expansion of the area under Soviet control. It is difficult to conceive of an adequate treatment of the Cold War that does not at least mention the essentially defensive character of the concept of containment.* It would also be appropriate to state, however, that from the Soviet point of view such a defensive perimeter established around Russia could be viewed as non-defensive in character.

Since Kennan was the principal conceptualizer of American foreign

*In terms of chronology, the "Truman Doctrine" was enunciated before Kennan's broader analysis and policy recommendation in the "X" article were published (March and June 1947, respectively). However, the Truman Doctrine, which was keyed to the situation in Greece and Turkey, is more usefully seen as a step in the implementation of the containment policy.

policy during the first two post-war decades, it would also be useful to state what effects he expected the containment policy to have. He wrote that the United States "has it in its power to increase enormously the strain under which Soviet policy must operate, to force upon the Kremlin a far greater degree of moderation and circumspection than it has had to observe in recent years, and in this way to promote tendencies which must eventually find their outlet in either the break-up or the gradual mellowing of Soviet power."

It would also be appropriate to state that Kennan later said that his policy proposal had been misunderstood and misapplied, that he had been most concerned over naïveté about Communism on the part of the American left, and that he had not anticipated that anti-Communists later would enshrine containment as a doctrine guiding American conduct in areas where in his opinion it was inapplicable.

Treatment

With the exception of textbook F, all the texts deal with or at least mention the policy of containment. Not always uncritically, of course. Textbook A, which sees the Cold War more as a struggle of ideas than as a power struggle (*"Ultimately, the Cold War involves the question of which system deserves to survive by offering the most opportunities for good lives"*), mentions containment in connection with the Truman Doctrine. The essential idea, it says, *"was to keep communism within its existing boundaries: to say to Moscow, and later to Peking as well, 'Thus far shall you go and no farther!' "* Textbook B, also in connection with the Truman Doctrine, gives containment one sentence. Neither of these treatments picks up the essence of Kennan's analysis of Soviet conduct or his assessment of the requirements of American security.

Textbook C gives the subject relatively sophisticated treatment. It summarizes part of the reasoning of the "X" article: *"He [Kennan] emphasized that Soviet leaders saw their relations with the West only in terms of antagonism, and he contended that they would continue to probe for weak spots in their drive to bring the downfall of capitalism. Though Kennan recognized circumstances could force a change in tactics, he argued the objectives of Soviet policy would remain constant unless the nature of Soviet power changed."* And textbook C then correctly quotes Kennan's key definition of containment.

While textbook C doesn't give an entirely satisfactory summary of Kennan's article (which spoke not of a "*drive* to bring about the downfall of capitalism" but rather of a natural tendency of Soviet power to flow into any vacuum), it does mention, to its credit, that Kennan himself subsequently changed his mind about the "X" article: "*Although several years later Kennan was to modify his views by insisting American leaders placed too much emphasis on military response, he did believe containment would weaken Soviet confidence in an ultimate Communist triumph. He also thought it would force Soviet leaders to moderate their objectives or face such strains on their power that the downfall of communism would result.*" A simplification of Kennan's views, perhaps, but textbook C offers a much more thoughtful treatment than the subject receives in the other five books.

Textbook D briefly mentions containment (defined as "commitments in order to prevent the Soviet Union and later the People's Republic of China from extending their power"), and it expresses skepticism in the form of a question at the margin: "*Why, if for any reason, should the United States try to stop other nations from expanding?*" It also mentions a 1952 statement of Kennan in which he argued that since in World War II one totalitarian power (Nazi Germany) could be defeated only with the help of another (the U.S.S.R.), it was inevitable that the U.S.S.R. would come to dominate half of Europe.

Textbook E introduces the subject of containment (in a commentary introducing an item of reading on NATO) in the following manner: "*Today, historians interested in the postwar period raise the question of why the United States developed the policy of containment to stop Communist aggression rather than make use of the United Nations, an organization created specifically to maintain peace.*" Having raised this question, which is not one hotly debated by historians, it lamely provides the answer: "*Possibly one of the reasons was that the UN lacked the power to prevent aggression by one of its leading members.*"

Textbook E then proceeds to offer a remarkable assortment of readings under the title "The Debate Over the Policy of Containment." It consists of (1) a speech by Vice-President Henry Wallace attacking the Truman Doctrine and containment as doing things that the U.N. should do; (2) a passage by John Foster Dulles attacking containment as a "negative policy [which] will never end the type of sustained offensive which the Soviet Union is mounting"; and (3) an excerpt from Walter

Lippmann arguing that the American temperament is unsuited to "a strategy of containing, waiting, countering, blocking, with no more specific objective than the eventual 'frustration' of the opponent." Three negative views—nobody is permitted to make a reasoned case *for* containment.

It is perhaps illustrative of the problems of the "inquiry" method that such deficiencies of the readings are compounded by the questions that textbook E puts to the pupil after he has been exposed to such an unbalanced diet. Since no explanation of containment was offered, there can of course be no question calling for such an explanation. The questions read: *"1. How do the three criticisms of the policy of containment challenge the statements by President Truman that you have seen? 2. How do the three critics of the policy of containment differ? 3. What alternative policies do the three critics propose? 4. What assumptions do these critics make about (a) the danger from the Soviet Union, (b) the proper use of American economic and military power?"* One wishes that another question had been asked: "Do you believe that on the basis of the readings in this book you have an adequate understanding of the reasoning behind the American policy of containment?"

Since textbook F did not mention Yalta or the Communist takeovers in Eastern Europe, one need not be surprised that it also gives its pupils nothing on the American debate about the containment of Communist expansion.

6
The Truman Doctrine

Criteria

Historians generally treat the Truman Doctrine as a major policy development on a par with the policy of containment, but one can also look upon Truman's speech of March 12, 1947, as a statement on implementation of the containment policy. It was enunciated in response to the urgent need to pick up from Great Britain the burden of supporting Greece and Turkey; but in applying containment to those countries the President also made a sweeping pronouncement (some say, too sweeping) that "it must be the policy of the United States to support free peoples who are resisting attempted subjugation by armed minorities or by outside pressure."

If one believes that the Truman Doctrine carried containment too far, it would be reasonable to show just what the President proposed and why it might have been excessive. Of course, one can also oppose both containment and the Truman Doctrine; or one can believe that the two are entirely compatible if one interprets the Truman 1947 speech as referring only to situations like that of Greece, where an armed Communist minority was able to defy a democratic government only because it was receiving supplies and sanctuary in neighboring Communist countries.

Treatment

All six textbooks mention the Truman Doctrine, though not all of them describe it accurately. For instance, textbook D says that "*the United States later expanded this so-called Truman Doctrine by promising to support any nation threatened by outside military pressure or armed aggression.*" The context makes it clear, however, that Truman did not have in mind merely "any" nation but specifically those that were threatened by Communist subversion or aggression.

Textbook E, whose "debate" over the policy of containment we have seen to be no debate at all, since it included only opponents of that policy, does give excerpts from the Truman March 12 speech (under a different heading), though some peculiar things have happened to it. For one thing, the key statement, "I believe it must be the policy of the United States to support free peoples who are resisting attempted subjugation by armed minorities or by outside pressures," does not appear in textbook E's two-page summarization.

Furthermore, a certain omission has taken place that can hardly be explained by space limitations. One key paragraph of the Truman speech is ever so slightly compressed, so that it reads: "The peoples of a number of countries of the world have recently had totalitarian regimes forced upon them against their will. The Government of the United States has made frequent protests against [aggression and force] . . . in Poland, Rumania, and Bulgaria. I must also state that in a number of other countries there have been similar developments."

Only someone who is familiar with the Truman speech and is left with a vague feeling that something is missing, could be expected to check this version against the original. And, lo and behold, where the three dots appear in textbook E, six words have been deleted: "in violation of the Yalta agreement." One must wonder whether the omission of two key points of this document occurred for reasons of space or for other reasons.

Textbook F contains a summary and brief comment on the Truman Doctrine—in fact, it offers the same comment twice. In summarizing the doctrine, textbook F says: *"The Presidential statement committed the United States to intervene in revolutions anywhere in the world. Some historians believe that Truman's policy was not wise. They feel that it drew the United States into situations over which American leaders had little or no control, and that Truman made no distinction between real military threats to American interests and revolutions which arose from local conditions."* And again, in introducing an excerpt of a Truman speech on a later page, textbook F says that the Truman Doctrine *"committed the United States to intervene in democratic revolutions occurring anywhere in the world. This intervention was supposed to keep other nations from coming under the influence of the Soviet Union."* The second comment differs from the first in that "democratic" is added before "revolutions." Presumably the authors (or editors?) assume that all revolutions are "democratic."

What is remarkable about the treatment of the Truman Doctrine by textbook F is not that the authors believe it to have been a mistake; many historians, including some of its authors and progenitors (like Kennan himself), believe that Truman carried containment too far, or with the wrong emphasis. The remarkable things about textbook F's treatment of this controversial subject are (1) that the negative comment distorts the content and underlying intent of the Doctrine (it did not "commit the United States to intervene in revolutions anywhere"); (2) that it mixes the comment in one instance into the same paragraph in which it provides truncated information about the Doctrine; and (3) that it rams its point home by reiteration. Even if one leaves out the elements of outright distortion, the pedagogic devices used suggest an attempt to indoctrinate the reader, particularly since the only quotation from a Truman speech (one he delivered two years after the Truman Doctrine, in 1949) is followed by these questions: *"When Truman made these remarks, the Cold War had already begun. What effect do you think this speech might have had on the tensions already built up by the Cold War? Do you think it might have eased them or made them worse?*'' Nothing is given to explain why Americans and other Western democratic peoples might have had reason in 1949 to fear the Soviet Union and the Communist assaults everywhere against the democracies.

When Truman set forth his Doctrine, the Greek Communists had mounted their third drive for power in three years, with the support of the Communist regimes of Albania, Yugoslavia, and Bulgaria. That fact is presented in this way by textbook F: ''*Great Britain tried to re-assert its influence in Greece by imposing a reactionary monarchy on the country. This action provoked a bitter civil war in Greece. Greek nationalists, led by Greek Communists and supported by the Communist governments of Yugoslavia and Bulgaria, waged a fierce guerrilla war in northern Greece. . . .*'' There are so many things wrong with this version of history that we must forgo detailed analysis. Suffice it to note that in the Greek elections of 1946, under the eyes of foreign observers including 692 Americans, a parliament was chosen that in its overwhelming majority—85 percent—supported the government against the subsequent Communist insurrection.

The only book of the six that contains a reasonably comprehensive treatment of arguments on both sides regarding containment and the Truman Doctrine is textbook C, which, as noted, also contains a fairly extensive quote from Kennan. Textbook C first summarizes the opposition of Vice-President Henry Wallace (''*he argued that the United States ought to direct its energies toward improving relations with the Soviet Union rather than adopting a containment policy which could only increase Soviet hostility*'') and the criticism of Walter Lippmann (''. . . *attacked the Truman Doctrine on the basis it assumed too great a responsibility in promising to aid free peoples everywhere, a responsibility which could result in an overextension of American power abroad. He rejected Kennan's thesis that Marxist ideology was the prime determinant of Soviet actions . . .*'').

Having presented these objections at some length, textbook C then gives the platform to a defender of containment and the Truman Doctrine, who is quoted as follows: ''The results of inaction were only too clear; the collapse of Europe's flank in the eastern Mediterranean, the establishment of Communist dominance in the Middle East, and a Soviet breakthrough into South Asia and North Africa. The psychological impact upon Europe of such a tremendous Soviet victory over the West would have been disastrous. For Europeans already psychologically demoralized by their sufferings and fall from power and prestige, this would have been the final blow. In short, what was at stake in Greece was America's survival itself." This quotation, set into the narrative text, may not be the most effective defense of the Truman Doctrine in view of its apocalyptic formulation, but it does help restore balance by giving the side of some of the American government's defenders.

7
The Berlin Blockade (1948-49) and the Berlin Wall (1961)

Criteria

The bare facts do *not* tell the Berlin story. The blockade started when the Soviet Union cut all overland access to West Berlin—located deep in the Soviet zone of occupation of Germany—in June 1948. The United States and Great Britain, unwilling to yield to such coercion, thereupon instituted a massive airlift to provide food, coal, and other supplies to the approximately two million people of West Berlin who did not want to come under the Communist yoke. The Soviet Union terminated the blockade in May 1949 when its failure had become apparent. Twelve years later, in 1961, after several other attempts to get the Western allies out of Berlin, the East German regime, a satellite of the Soviet Union, erected a wall between East and West Berlin. Without the political context, these events are difficult to understand. On the other hand, a detailed exposition of that political context would require several paragraphs.

The Russian moves with respect to Berlin must be seen against the background of the original agreement of 1944 that provided for joint (Soviet and Western) administration of Germany (East and West) by an Allied Control Council sitting in Berlin. The city was also to be administered jointly by a body subordinate to the council. As disagreements over reparations and economic policies in the Eastern and Western zones of Germany could not be resolved, the Western powers (the United States, Great Britain, and France) decided in 1948 to unite their three zones into one entity, which later became the German Federal Republic. The U.S.S.R. blockaded Berlin in the hope of forestalling that move. All four powers paid lip service to the idea of unifying Germany, but each of them had reasons to fear unification, especially under circumstances favoring the other side.

The problem of Berlin was aggravated in 1948 by the Western intention to introduce the West German currency into West Berlin, which was not then and is not now a part of West Germany. The blockade of West Berlin was accompanied by violent tactics of the East German Communist Party (called the Socialist Unity Party) against the leading party of West Berlin, the staunchly democratic Socialist Party, which had refused appeals for "unity" with the Communists.

Once West Germany had become an economic and political reality, the Soviet Union sought to promote equal status for East Germany and an end to the Western military presence in Berlin. One means of forcing such an outcome would have been for the Soviets to conclude a "peace treaty" with East Germany. But East Germany was regarded as a kind of Russian colony by the West German government. The Soviet Union at various times issued ultimatums or near-ultimatums to the West. In 1961, Premier Khrushchev tried to intimidate President Kennedy at their meeting in Vienna; the President replied by calling for an increase in American arms and by warning the Soviet Union not to tamper with Western rights in Berlin.

Another important element in the situation—obviously, not all such elements can be mentioned in a cursory treatment of the Berlin problem—was the fact, which continues to this day, that West Berlin with its political and economic freedoms was a constant embarrassment and irritant to East Germany, which surrounds it. The border between West and East Berlin was the only place in the so-called Iron Curtain where people could still travel relatively freely between Eastern and Western Europe. Hundreds of thousands of East Germans used that exit route to seek refuge in free and economically prosperous West Germany. Erection of the wall in 1961 put an end to what had become a hemorrhage of skilled labor leaving East Germany.

Treatment

Textbook A gives one paragraph to the Berlin airlift and three paragraphs to the continuing difficulties over Berlin in later years. The treatment of the blockade provides no background: "*In the summer of 1948, the USSR tried to starve the Western powers out of Berlin by stopping all traffic from West Germany. The western allies overcame the Berlin blockade by an 'air lift', whereby supplies for over two million people were flown to the German capital. Hour after hour, day after day, for over a year, American and British cargo planes carried food, medical supplies, clothing, even coal, to the German capital. In May 1949, Russia lifted the blockade. 'When we refused to be forced out of the city of Berlin,' wrote Truman, 'we demonstrated to the people of Europe that with their cooperation we would act, and act resolutely, when their freedom was threatened.'* '' Nothing here about the Russian reasons for the blockade.

The treatment of the later crises contains more interpretation. In connection with the fifties, textbook A notes that ''*West Berlin was a continuing reproach to the USSR because it was so much more prosperous than the eastern sector of the city held by the Communists. Moreover, it provided a route through which hundreds of thousands of people escaped from East Germany. Khrushchev repeatedly said that the situation was 'intolerable' and tried to frighten the West into backing down. But the Western alliance firmly refused all compromise on the issue of the freedom of West Berlin or the right of free access along the transportation routes connecting the city with West Germany.*''

With respect to the events of 1961, textbook A is the only one to refer to the Kennedy-Khrushchev meeting in Vienna: ''*Perhaps thinking that he could intimidate the young President who had recently emerged from the Bay of Pigs fiasco with a damaged reputation, Khrushchev handed Kennedy a near-ultimatum on East Germany and Berlin. He insisted that the Western powers recognize the Russian puppet state and that the four-power occupation of Berlin be ended. When the President refused, the Communist answer was a wall across Berlin, barring free movement between their district and the rest of the city. . . . It closed off the flight of refugees from East Germany. . . . 'The Wall' was visible testimony that the 'people's democracy' of East Germany was a vast prison.*'' This treatment, while it editorializes more than most of the others, is the only one that explains precisely what Khrushchev wanted; why he did not get it; and how the building of the wall brought the situation in Berlin into conformity with the rigid separation of East and West in the rest of Europe.

Textbook B mentions Berlin three times: once in reporting the barebones facts about the blockade; once in relating the Soviet ultimatum to the Western powers in 1958; and finally in a somewhat more explicit statement of Soviet desires (but not motivations) in connection with the threat made by Khrushchev in 1961: *"He warned that the treaty* [*with East Germany*] *would end the Western nations' rights of free access to West Berlin. President Kennedy in turn warned that the United States would not abandon the people of West Berlin. . . ."*

The description of the end of the blockade in 1949 is inaccurate: *"The British-American answer to the Soviet challenge was the Berlin airlift. . . . This crisis in East-West relations was finally resolved with the aid of the U.N."* The crisis was not resolved with the aid of the United Nations. An American journalist asked Stalin whether he would end the blockade "if the governments of the United States, the United Kingdom and France agreed to postpone the establishment of a separate West German state pending a meeting of the Council of Foreign Ministers to consider the question of Germany as a whole." Stalin's reply was that "the Soviet Government sees no obstacles to lifting transport restrictions [under the stated conditions] on the understanding that transport and trade restrictions by the three powers [the so-called counter-blockade against East Germany] should be lifted simultaneously."

Thereupon the U.S. permanent representative to the United Nations (Philip Jessup) was instructed to ask the Soviet permanent representative (Yakov Malik) whether Stalin's omission of the currency matter had been accidental. One month later, Malik told Jessup that it had not been accidental, whereupon agreement was reached on a face-saving formula that allowed the Soviets to lift the blockade. The fact that the American inquiry took place at the U.N. headquarters does not justify attributing resolution of the crisis to "the aid of the U.N." As we shall see, this is not the only instance where textbook B builds up the image of the United Nations when the facts do not justify it.

Textbook C devotes 1½ pages to the deadlock over Germany and the Berlin Blockade, explaining that the Russians were reacting to Western moves to consolidate their zones: *"The Russians reacted by creating a crisis in Berlin, with the probable objective of compelling the western powers to abandon their plan for a West German state."* The initial moves and countermoves until the blockade became complete are recounted, and textbook C even explains the connection with the currency reform: *"The Berlin crisis soon became linked with a currency dispute when the western powers proceeded with a plan to provide the West Germans with sound money by replacing inflated occupation currency with new marks. . . . Soviet opposition to currency reform, mainly because it exposed the unsoundness of the East mark, became apparent during discussion of the blockade. The Soviet Union offered to reopen the approaches to Berlin if the western powers called off the currency change-over.*" This is not entirely accurate: Stalin had offered to end the blockade if the Western powers accepted the East German mark in West Berlin—but it is probably too much to expect a high school textbook to go into such details.

Despite its copious treatment of Germany and Berlin, textbook C does not explain why the Russians had the wall built in 1961. It merely says: "*Conflict between the two blocs in the 1960's tended to follow the 'oscillating line' pattern of the late 1950's. In a test of wills over Berlin in 1961, for example, the line hardened as Kennedy insisted that the rights of West Berliners to free access to West Germany be protected. The Soviets and East Germans then increased Cold War tensions by building a wall between the two halves of the city.*" This makes it appear that Western refusal to capitulate forced the Russians to build the wall. The massive exodus from East Germany through Berlin is not mentioned.

Textbook D compresses the German problem, the Berlin blockade, the airlift, and the wall into one paragraph. It explains that the Western powers announced plans in 1948 for the creation of a West German state. "*The Soviets reacted to this announcement and to the success of the Marshall Plan by blockading the roads to Berlin in June 1948. When the Soviets refused to let allied convoys into Berlin, the citizens of West Berlin faced starvation. Any allied attempt to break through the blockade might mean war with the Soviet Union. The Allies solved the crisis by bringing in supplies by air. In May 1949, the U.S.S.R. lifted the blockade. But Berlin continued to play a potentially explosive role in the Cold War. Thousands of refugees from the Soviet zone of the city fled to the allied zone. In order to halt the flow of refugees, Soviet Premier Nikita Khrushchev had a wall built in 1961 along the line dividing the city.*"

Textbook F wins the prize for brevity. On the blockade and airlift (it has nothing on the wall) it has this to say: "*1948. Berlin Airlift. In June 1948, the Soviet government threw up a blockade around Berlin, cutting the city off from all overland traffic from the West. The United States and Great Britain airlifted food and coal to the blockaded area.*

A year later the Soviet Union ended the blockade." This, of course, explains nothing.

Textbook E, which like textbook F relies mainly on documentary readings, has nothing on the blockade, airlift, or wall.

8
The United Nations and the Cold War

Criteria

One can be enthusiastic or skeptical about the United Nations, but it would not be fair to the reader to describe its elaborate organization without any comment, for that could convey the mistaken impression that the United Nations has the capacity to govern major international events. Any adequate description of the United Nations must point out at least some of the following salient facts about the organization: that the Security Council cannot act against the negative vote of one of its five permanent members; that this feature of the Charter was not the result of Russian obstinacy but had been desired also by the United States; that the resolutions of the General Assembly are not binding upon the membership; that, on the other hand, the moral force of the organization can be considerable in certain circumstances; and that many practical benefits derive from the activities of the U.N.'s specialized organizations. To describe the United Nations as a world parliament would do both it and the reader a disservice, for too much would then be expected of it. On the other hand, a balanced description of the United Nations would give credit to its limited capabilities for peacekeeping, pointing out, however, that this role could be played only when it suited the interests of all five permanent Security Council members.

Treatment

All six textbooks give essential information about the United Nations, often with some background about the issues that had to be resolved in its formation, and usually with more or less lengthy descriptions of its organization. However, as might be expected, there are significant differences in approach and in the optimism the textbooks reflect about the U.N.'s capability to prevent world conflicts.

Textbook A makes it clear from the beginning that since each permanent member has a veto, "*the Security Council would be effective only so long as the wartime cooperation of the 'big five' continued. In other words, the UN was powerless to act if a single major power decided to prevent it.*" At another place, in describing the Communist world outlook, textbook A says: " '*To the Communists,' writes a recent observer, 'the UN is no more than an instrument of conflict', rather than an agency for international cooperation.*" This illustrates the general tone. Textbook A has half a page on "UN Failures" and half a page on "UN Achievements," but it takes the position that in security matters "*. . . American expectations were . . . somewhat exaggerated since the UN lacked power to enforce its decisions and in some situations even lacked the power to make a decision.*"

Textbook B takes a more sanguine view of the organization, which it describes in greater detail, with charts and other aids. It quotes, with evident approval, President Truman's statement in 1945: "This Charter points down the only road to enduring peace. There is no other." Yet it notes that the organization was unable to prevent, or even to mitigate, conflicts between the two super-powers. (That the Western European democracies are also participants in the Cold War is usually downplayed if not ignored. The Cold War, as a headline in textbook B puts it, was or is "Between the United States and the U.S.S.R.")

Textbook B brings in the United Nations whenever it had a role in abating world tensions, and even sometimes when it didn't. For instance, in reporting the outbreak of fighting between Jews and Arabs during the formation of the state of Israel in 1948, it says: "*The UN at once took steps to end the fighting*"—as if those steps, rather than the military realities, had brought the result. We noted in section 7 that textbook B gives undeserved credit to the United Nations for helping to resolve the Berlin crisis in 1949. In connection with the Korean War, it states that "*in response to the UN's call, President Truman ordered the United States Seventh Fleet to prevent any attack upon Formosa and to blockade the Korean coast*"—which is something that was done unilaterally by the United States. In describing the situation brought about by Israel, Great Britain, and France in their attack on Egypt in 1956, textbook B notes that these allies of the U.S. "*had ignored the UN*"—as if this had been the source of the American embarrassment. Again, the withdrawal of American troops from Lebanon and British troops from Jordan in 1958 is said to have taken place *"after the Secretary General of the UN reported that the situation was improving"*—a post-hoc-ergo-propter-hoc fallacy probably inspired by a desire to give a boost to the world organization.

Textbook C is more analytical than descriptive about the organization of the United Nations and the difficulties that attended its creation. Its point of view is perhaps epitomized by the sentence, *"It was obvious from the start that the success of the U.N. was dependent on the major powers' cooperation."*

Textbook D gives the United Nations cursory treatment but mentions that any of the five permanent Security Council members could veto action.

Textbook E devotes seventeen pages to readings and other material on the United Nations. There are lengthy selections from speeches by President Roosevelt, Senator Tom Connally, the isolationist Senator Burton Wheeler, and a biographer of Senator Arthur Vandenberg; an analysis of the Charter by Professor Arthur Link; citations from the Charter itself; and "an optimistic view" and "a pessimistic view" by a journalist and the Australian foreign minister, respectively.

Textbook E is the one that, in dealing with containment, had raised the question why the United States could not have relied on the United Nations to forestall any Soviet aggression (and remarked that "possibly" the reason was that the U.N. lacked the power to do this). It is also the textbook that carries the long discussion of the dangers of bias that we noted in chapter 1. Curiously, that warning is found in connection with textbook E's treatment of the United Nations. Having exhorted the reader to guard against bias, it says: *"The report on the first United Nations meetings you have just read is a statement with a bias. It seems clear that the reporter wanted his readers to know his bias."* And there follow various questions about the bias of the writer, a whimsical journalist who saw the first sessions of the U.N. on Flushing Meadow as "the little flower of man's hope that blooms precariously where New York once burned its refuse."

Textbook F gives two readings, one for and one against the United Nations, dating from 1945. Neither is particularly illuminating, especially since the speech favoring U.N. membership stresses the provision for a U.N. "police force to put down aggression," which was never implemented.

9
The Korean War (1950-53)

Criteria

Although the Communists still maintain that South Korea attacked North Korea on June 25, 1950, there is really no argument among serious historians: it was the other way around. The significance of the event, however, is subject to many differing interpretations. A fair exposition should recall that, rightly or wrongly, the unprovoked Communist aggression in Korea was considered at the time as signaling a Communist intention to challenge the non-Communist world also in other areas, perhaps even in Europe. Accordingly, policy-makers in Washington as well as in Western Europe considered it essential to let the Communists know that such crossings of the demarcation line between East and West would be resolutely resisted.

The U.S. response to the North Korean attack went beyond containment. No treatment of the Korean War would be adequate if it did not explain the significance of the decision of the United Nations—taken under American influence—to push the invaders back beyond the thirty-eighth parallel, the boundary line between North and South Korea, toward the boundary between North Korea and China. This decision, which in effect involved an attempted "rollback" of the Communists, led to the entry of China into the war. The war ended in 1953 where it could have ended two years earlier, near the old boundary between North and South Korea.

Treatment

All six textbooks mention the Korean War, though some only briefly, and none takes the Communist position that South Korea started the conflict. Textbook A considers that the North Korean invasion "*provided a vital test for the UN,*" which is a bit odd, since it was only the fortuitous circumstance of the Soviet representative's absence from the Security Council that permitted the U.N. umbrella to be put over the American military response to Communist aggression.

Textbook B reports the accident of the absence of the Soviet representative and correctly notes that "*although 19 UN members finally contributed assistance, the major burden of defending South Korea fell on the United States.*'' The same text states, as already noted, that it was ''in response to the UN's call'' that President Truman ordered the Seventh Fleet to defend Taiwan (and fails to note that the fleet was also ordered to prevent attacks from Taiwan on the Chinese mainland).

Textbook C devotes three full pages to the war. It is the only one to flag the policy importance of the decision, after the American counterthrust at Inchon, to carry the war north of the thirty-eighth parallel. (''*To pursue the fleeing North Korean army across the 38th parallel for the purpose of destroying its military capability would have changed the character of the war from a defensive to offensive action.*'') Actually, the crossing of the thirty-eighth parallel had not only military but also declared political objectives. Textbook C, while it speculates that the North Korean attack may have reflected a desire of the Communists to ''test containment,'' does not call the reader's attention to the argument—indeed, the fact—that the decision to advance northward beyond the thirty-eighth parallel was in fundamental contradiction to the containment policy. It is surprising that texts that in other respects are rather free in quoting critics of American policy are almost silent on this important and controversial point.

Textbook D says on the matter only: ''[General] MacArthur requested that he be permitted to pursue the North Koreans toward the Chinese border. President Truman consented.'' The disastrous aftermath is related but not analyzed.

However, textbook E, which consists mostly of readings, highlights an angle that is illuminated nowhere else when it quotes Senator Robert Taft as pointing out in 1950 that the United States had in effect washed its hands of South Korea when it had withdrawn its troops the previous year. ''Korea itself is not vitally important to the United States,'' the senator is quoted as saying. ''It is hard to defend. We have another instance of communism picking out a soft spot where the Communists feel that they can make a substantial advance and can obtain a moral victory without risking war. From the past philosophy and declarations of our leaders, it was not unreasonable for the North Koreans to suppose that they could get away with it and that we would do nothing about it.''

Textbook E also has another unusual feature—a long quotation, in the form of a reading, from the work of one of the authors of the textbook itself. That quotation, three pages of it, may be taken to represent the conclusions that are being suggested. The decision to go north of the thirty-eighth parallel is termed "fateful" because it led to the Chinese counterinvasion. There is an account of how the blessing of the United Nations was secured (through the General Assembly, to avoid a Soviet veto). In the end it is stated that "the Truman administration was forced to retreat to the original political goal of the war—the containment of North Korean aggression."

"All in all," this item in textbook E concludes, "the Korean War was a frustrating experience for Americans. The war had cost 25,604 dead, 103,492 wounded, and over 10,000 missing only to end in the *status quo ante bellum*. The economic costs were also very great; defense expenditures rose from $11.9 billion in 1950 to $43.6 billion in 1953, and a huge military establishment seemed to be installed as a permanent feature of the national economy." There is no suggestion that restoration of the *status quo ante bellum* was an important and legitimate objective that might have been worth the sacrifice in order to deter future wars of Communist aggression.

It will be recalled (see sections 5 and 8) that textbook E raised the question why the United States, instead of adopting a policy of containment, did not "*make use* [*instead*] *of the United Nations, the organization created specifically to maintain peace.*" It is interesting that this textbook, while it tells its readers that the United Nations "*meeting in emergency session . . . adopted resolutions condemning the invasion and calling upon UN members to give all necessary assistance to South Korea,*" does not explain that this action of the Security Council was fortuitous, because of the absence of its Soviet member.

Textbook F has by far the most unsatisfactory treatment of the Korean War, not because of bias but because it entirely skips over the causes of the Chinese counterinvasion: "*The United Nations also* [*sic*] *sent an international force to Korea to work with the American and South Korean armies under the command of General Douglas MacArthur. The Chinese army entered the war on the side of North Korea.*" Brief though its treatment is, textbook F like textbook E succeeds in leaving the reader with a sense of total futility of the effort to defend South Korea: "*The boundary of North and South Korea remained at the 38th parallel, and Korea remained divided into two hostile camps.*" Since it is also detailed that the war cost more than 54,000 American lives and over $22 billion, the reader is led to the conclusion that the entire effort must be judged a failure, rather than a defensive success flawed by the ill-considered attempt to "roll back" the adversary.

(It is inevitable that in large surveys of this kind some factual errors will occur, so normally we note these only when they seem to reflect a pedagogical device or political point of view. However, in this instance the reader must be wondering whether textbook E's figure of 25,604 American dead or textbook F's figure of 54,000 is correct. Neither is. According to the U.S. Department of Defense, the number of Americans who died in the Korean War was 33,629. This includes 4,735 declared to be "presumed dead" under the Missing Persons Act. Textbook authors generally do not work with primary sources.)

10

McCarthy and Anti-Communism in the 1950s

Criteria

"McCarthyism" is still an emotionally charged subject today, almost thirty years after the junior senator from Wisconsin launched himself into prominence on the basis of unjustified accusations of treason in high places. The difficulty lies in presenting the subject in a manner that makes the success of Joseph McCarthy understandable. That he was a demagogue is no longer disputed. But what accounted for the toleration of his excesses? Was he an irrational aberration, or did he reflect—or pander to—a justified concern about American internal-security problems? Even today, some people find it difficult even to discuss such questions, seeing McCarthyism as essentially an assault on "dissent."

An adequate description of the McCarthy period might sketch the historical context; it might discuss the fall of China to the Communists and shortly thereafter the Korean War, both exploited by some politicians as having been facilitated by treason in high places. A treatment of the period should also make plain the reality of certain threats to American security as brought out by the espionage cases of Alger Hiss, Julius and Ethel Rosenberg, and (abroad) Klaus Fuchs and Bruno Pontecorvo. There was a widespread belief that without the help of Communist agents who had infiltrated into Western governments, the Russians could not have achieved the production of their own atomic bomb when they did, only four years after World War II.

Treatment of the McCarthy period might also mention the long silence of leaders of his own party, including President Eisenhower, in the face of the senator's transgressions; and the fact that it was possible to be strongly against McCarthy, yet equally strongly against allowing Communists in sensitive positions in the government.

Treatment

The textbooks either provide overly copious and one-sided presentations, or fall into the other extreme by not mentioning the subject at all, except in a very general way in connection with a political backlash in the United States after the "loss" of China in 1949 and the war in Korea.

Textbooks D and E do not mention Senator McCarthy at all, although the former does refer to backlash after the defeat of the Chinese Nationalists under Chiang Kai-shek.

Textbook A is very severe in its condemnation of McCarthyism, mentioning that he "*declared that the Democratic Party was guilty of 'twenty years of treason' in the course of which Roosevelt had deliberately sacrificed the fleet at Pearl Harbor to get the United States into war, and had sold out to Russia at Yalta. McCarthy claimed to have lists of 205, or 57, or 81 'card-carrying Communists' in the State Department. While not one of these was ever discovered and a Senate committee declared the charges were 'a fraud and a hoax', in the atmosphere of the time McCarthy enjoyed an ever-increasing influence.*"

"*The new witch-hunting,*" textbook A continues, "*went far beyond the federal government. Private vigilante groups sought to pin the Communist label on liberal and reformist people in every walk of life. They were successful in driving allegedly 'pink' professors from universities, in getting supposedly subversive textbooks banned from schools, and in blackballing certain broadcasters and entertainers from television, as well as actors from the stage and films.*" What is missing here is any reference to the fact that the United States had reason to be concerned about espionage. (There are of course some people who still want to believe that *all* people accused of espionage were victims of "McCarthyism," but they are a small minority among historians.) In any case, textbook A should not be faulted for skimping on such reasons for concern that contributed to the success of McCarthy, since it is the only one among the six that, in an earlier passage dealing with Communism, points out that Communists were tightly organized, often concealed their political allegiance, and were obedient to a foreign power: "*Unquestioning party members, and their dupes,*" it tells its readers, "*are willing, on order from Moscow or Peking, to engage in spying, sabotage, and the promotion of unrest.*"

Textbook B treats the subject more gingerly, in connection with increasing concern in the United States about Communist espionage as the Cold War became more acute: "*In its deepening concern over internal security, Congress was reacting not only to the possibility of Communist subversion at home but also to the increasingly serious international situation. Both of these issues played major roles in the Presidential election of 1952.*" And later: "*The Eisenhower administration also inherited a difficult problem of constitutional rights. Congressional committees were sometimes accused of handling individuals suspected of subversion without proper regard for fair judicial practices. The most controversial was a subcommittee headed by Senator Joseph McCarthy of Wisconsin.*"

Textbook C manages to compress the whole story into one paragraph, with a distinct point of view, as follows: "*One of the major results of the Korean War was an increasing conviction on the part of many American leaders and the public at large that the struggle against communism was total and global. This nation's commitment to South Vietnam came as a result of the Korean War, as did the decision by the Eisenhower administration to defend Quemoy and Matsu as part of Taiwan. The chief domestic result was McCarthyism, the unleashing of extremism in ferreting out alleged subversives responsible for the nation's supposed weakness in the face of Communist aggression. No individual, even the highest officials in government or the most noted scholars, were exempt from the threats and slurs of McCarthy. The resulting climate of general fear and uncertainty perhaps contributed to the public's acceptance of the nation's aggressive military policies in Southeast Asia.*"

One might argue about the point of view of textbook C, but there is clearly here an effort to compress many thoughts into one paragraph and not to labor any particular point. A diplomatic analyst might point out, for instance, that America's commitment to the defense of South

Vietnam came long after the Korean War and that support of the French military effort in Southeast Asia in the early 1950s was also motivated by our desire to see France accept the rearmament of Germany within the framework of the European Defense Community. It is also debatable whether American policy in Southeast Asia can be fairly described as "aggressive," since it served distinctly defensive purposes. However, here we enter onto historical territory that is so close to the present that dispassionate analysis is especially difficult.

Textbook F devotes to the McCarthy phenomenon a generous twelve pages out of twenty-eight treating the Cold War. (An additional nineteen pages, of which fifteen and a half are devoted to Vietnam, deal with foreign-policy events after 1960. Of the twenty-eight pages in the Cold War chapter, three, as we noted earlier, deal with Marx, Lenin, and Russia up to World War II.) The treatment consists almost entirely of readings.

The first reading acknowledges the origin of the McCarthy period, which lay in legitimate security concerns that became exaggerated. "Espionage and treason were one thing. Loyalty was quite another. It was extremely difficult to deal with the question of loyalty in America . . . because difference of opinion and criticism of established institutions were marks of a free society." This implies that any examination of a person's loyalty to the United States is in itself a violation of that person's civil rights. The Hiss case is put in these terms: "One especially disturbing case in the late 1940's was that of Alger Hiss. . . . Many people found it hard to believe that Hiss could ever have betrayed his country. . . . The full story of Hiss continues to elude the historian even today. . . . But Hiss trapped himself by telling a strange tale full of contradictions. After two dramatic trials he was sent to prison for perjury. . . ."

Few young people know anything today about Alger Hiss. At the time of the affair, American liberals could not bring themselves to believe, despite the evidence, that Hiss was guilty of espionage, simply because the people who accused him were politically so unappealing; and this seems to be true also of textbook F. The whole question whether a government has the right to protect itself from disloyal personnel in sensitive positions has been beclouded by the phenomenon of McCarthyism, defined as *unfair* accusations against *innocent* people—as if there had never been Communists who put loyalty to the Soviet Union above loyalty to their own country, and as if Communists had never been given the task of concealing their allegiance and infiltrating positions in democratic governments. Because of his wild exaggerations, McCarthy managed to discredit anti-Communism; and his memory continues to be used to discredit even legitimate security concerns.

There are colorful passages in the readings in textbook F showing the length to which anti-Communist hysteria went during the McCarthy period; for instance: ". . . State governments, businesses, universities, and small-town vigilante groups joined in [McCarthy's] crusade to purge the nation of Communists and their sympathizers. On the floor of [one state] legislature one member proposed that the wearing of six-shooters be legalized as a means of cleaning out the Communists and 'pinkos'. But the legislature settled for requiring every man, woman, and child who was in any way connected with a publicly supported school or other institution to sign an oath testifying to his loyalty and swearing that he had never been a Communist." The implication, clearly, is that because the search for Communists *everywhere* was ridiculous and dangerous, the search for Communists *anywhere* was equally ridiculous and dangerous.

The confusion between indiscriminate witch-hunting and legitimate screening of people in positions requiring high confidence is carried to its final extreme by the insertion of a comment, by the authors of textbook F, between two items of reading on McCarthy: "*Conformity v. Dissent in American Life. The views and actions of Senator McCarthy raised several important issues for Americans. One of the most important centered around the right of Americans to dissent, or freely express opinions which differed from those held by the majority. The right to freely express opinions on any subject is guaranteed by the First Amendment to the Constitution. It states. . . . Americans who opposed Senator McCarthy felt that his views and actions were endangering the rights protected by the First Amendment. They felt that dissent was vital to a free society. Those who supported Senator McCarthy believed that dissent was bad for America. They believed that it would undermine and weaken American society and lead to its takeover by Communists. . . .*" But this was not the position of those who supported Senator McCarthy, misguided though they may have been. The problem with them was that they saw Communists under every bed and suspected them to have secretly infiltrated into decision-making positions in the government, into the teaching profession, into the performing arts, and so on. Some such infiltration had in fact taken place, though its extent was exaggerated.

Textbook F, when it then asks the student at the end of the chapter to explain, "*What does it mean to dissent? To conform?,*" implies that that is what McCarthyism was about.

11
Castro's Rise to Power

Criteria

Historians generally agree that the government of General Fulgencio Batista was dictatorial, corrupt, inefficient, and overly accommodating toward American corporations. It is also generally agreed that Fidel Castro, leading a tiny band of guerrillas to victory, met with the approval of many Cubans who hoped that Batista's regime would be followed by democratic government. An adequate treatment of what happened in Cuba should explain how and why Castro, who initially was probably not a Communist (although Communists were among his close advisers), came into conflict with the United States and moved to closer and closer relations with the Soviet Union. Part of the difficulties between the United States and the Castro government had to do with the activities of Cuban refugees in the United States. A description of Castro's rise to power and drift toward Communism is not easily accomplished in a short summary, but it is essential as background for treatment of the Bay of Pigs invasion of 1961 and the Cuban missile crisis of 1962.

Treatment

Superficially, the various treatments may seem similar; but as will be seen, there are significant differences.

Textbook A says that "*the corrupt and ruthless government of General Fulgencio Batista faced a rebellion headed by the radical Fidel Castro. The United States stopped all aid to Batista, an action which helped Castro and his bearded followers toward victory; they entered Havana on January 1, 1959. Castro was generally popular in the United States. But enthusiasm for the new government waned as the*

Cuban leader began to denounce the United States, to confiscate private property, and to seek the friendship and military support of Russia and Red China. . . ." There follows a brief recitation of events and trends that led to the complete break in relations.

Textbook B states: "*The Kennedy administration also inherited the extremely serious problem of Cuba. Early in 1959 guerrilla forces led by Fidel Castro overthrew the government of Cuban dictator Fulgencio Batista (bah-TEES-tah). And at first the United States welcomed Castro's rise to power as a victory for democracy. American sympathy rapidly faded, however, when Castro began to act like a ruthless dictator. He failed to hold the elections he had promised. He put to death hundreds of political enemies and jailed thousands unsympathetic to his regime. He took control of foreign-owned property. In addition, Castro began to lash out at 'Yankees' and to turn to Communist nations for support. Castro accepted a Soviet offer of military aid if the United States interfered in Cuba.*"

Textbook C, as usual, is somewhat more thorough, devoting three paragraphs to the same development: "*Between 1933 and 1959 Cuba was ruled by military dictator Fulgencio Batista. Economically Cuba was dominated by American corporations, and diplomatically it followed this nation's hemispheric policies. Since many Cubans regarded Batista as a representative of the American government, the successful overthrow of Batista by Fidel Castro in 1959 was seen in part as an anti-American revolution.*

"*Castro's rise to power did not, however, lead to an immediate break with the United States. Castro had, in fact, received considerable aid from private American sources during the guerrilla war waged against Batista, and his regime was quickly recognized by Eisenhower. Even after mass public trials and execution of Batista supporters and other opponents, which offended many Americans' sense of justice, Castro was favorably received during a trip to the United States. Therefore, at the start of his rule, the possibilities for an American accommodation seemed to be strong.*

"*But the deterioration of relations between Cuba and the United States quickly developed. The deterioration stemmed chiefly from misinterpretation of and exaggerations about each other's motives. While the Castro regime interpreted American actions and policies as threats to Cuban sovereignty, American leaders saw Cuban actions as undermining the nation's hemispheric policy.*" There follows an account of the sequence of events that led to the break in relations, including the blowing up of a French munitions ship in Havana's harbor, which Castro blamed on American intelligence agents; the nationalization of American business firms; Eisenhower's cutting of Cuba's quota of sugar imports into the United States; the arrival of Soviet technicians in Cuba; and Castro's proclamation of his allegiance to "Marxism."

Textbook D says: "*In 1959, Fidel Castro led a successful revolution to overthrow the government of Fulgencio Batista. The Batista government was one of the most corrupt and dictatorial regimes in the Western hemisphere. President Eisenhower quickly granted diplomatic recognition to the Castro government. Castro, however, was violently anti-American. He harangued the United States in long speeches. He seized American-owned property without adequate compensation. And he openly courted the support of the Soviet Union as he set up a Communist state in Cuba.*"

Textbook E: "*In 1959 a revolution in Cuba led by Fidel Castro overthrew the harsh military dictatorship of Fulgencio Batista. After assuming control of the government, Castro took over American property in Cuba and proceeded to introduce far-reaching social and economic reforms. Angered at the high-handed actions of Castro's government toward American citizens and property, President Eisenhower broke off diplomatic relations with Cuba. Castro, in turn, turned to the Soviet Union for economic aid and publicly announced that the Cuban government was to pursue a policy of close alignment with the Communist nations of the world.*"

Textbook F: "*On January 1, 1959, a young nationalist leader, Fidel Castro, ousted the corrupt Cuban dictator, Fulgencio Batista. Although Castro himself was not a Communist, his closest advisers were. Gradually, Cuba was transformed into a Marxist society. Castro made sweeping changes within Cuban society. For example, extensive farmlands were taken away from a few immensely rich families and redistributed to the poor Cubans who had been working them. Castro also attempted to wipe out widespread hunger by rationing food and to abolish illiteracy. Many of these changes—especially Castro's seizure of American-owned properties—angered the United States. By 1960 relations between Cuba and the United States had completely deteriorated.*"

On cursory reading, these summaries may have seemed fairly similar; but their differences are more significant than their similarities. All texts mention that Castro's predecessor was a dictator, and all deal with Castro's confiscation of American property. But E and F fail to mention that American attitudes toward Castro were initially favorable, and only textbooks B and C deal with Castro's failure to hold elections and his harshness in dealing with political opponents. On the other hand, textbooks E and F, which turn a blind eye to the lack of democratic liberties under Castro, are the only ones to mention social and economic reforms, with textbook F creating the totally erroneous impression that the lands "redistributed to the poor Cubans who had been working them" were then actually owned by them. Instead, they were collectivized. There was also no "widespread hunger" in Cuba until the collectivization took place, and it was not "wiped out" by food rationing.

12

The Bay of Pigs (1961) and the Cuban Missile Crisis (1962)

Criteria

President Kennedy took personal responsibility for the fiasco of the Bay of Pigs invasion in 1961, remarking that "success has many fathers, but failure is an orphan." It would be fair to state that he had inherited the preparations for the ill-fated operation from his predecessor. It would also be fair to state that he scaled down overt American participation to the point where it made failure much more likely. No doubt the most important reason for the failure of the landing of Cuban refugees, however, was inadequate American intelligence. It was apparently believed that the Castro regime was so unpopular that there would be a spontaneous uprising among the Cuban people. Also, it was apparently not anticipated that the immediate rounding up and incarceration of potential supporters of the expedition would be so effective. The Cuban exile force, bereft of air support and resupply, was quickly surrounded by Cuban forces and, pleading in vain for American help, killed or captured in its entirety.

The missile crisis of 1962 was not unrelated to the Bay of Pigs, since the introduction of Soviet offensive missiles into Cuba probably appeared to the Communists as a measure to deter an American invasion. This involved a failure of Russian intelligence, for the American reaction to the clandestine installation of Soviet nuclear missiles on America's doorstep almost precipitated the very invasion the missiles were presumably designed to deter. An adequate treatment should point out how President Kennedy decided against courses of action that would have made a Russian retreat more difficult, and how the "quarantine" of Cuba was designed to give the Soviet leadership time to back away from a confrontation. The sequence of moves and countermoves during the crisis was complicated. If one describes them in any detail, one cannot go by a simple chronology.

Treatment

All the textbooks have the essentials of the Bay of Pigs story, but some comment more perceptively than others on the connection between the Bay of Pigs, which was a case of indirect American aggression, and the Cuban Missile Crisis, which involved a direct projection of Soviet power into the Western hemisphere. Textbook A, after summarizing the fiasco, says: "*The appalling failure of this 'invasion by proxy' was a heavy blow to the prestige of the new Kennedy administration: Castro was strengthened in power; Khrushchev posed as the defender of Latin America against the 'Colossus of the North'; there were anti-United States riots in Latin-American cities.*"

Textbook B, more significantly, notes: "*Following the Bay of Pigs invasion attempt, the Soviet Union stepped up its shipments of military equipment to Cuba. In December 1961 Castro declared publicly, 'I am a Marxist-Leninist and will be one until the day I die.'* "

Textbook C says: "*In the tense days which followed the Bay of Pigs fiasco, Khrushchev pledged to defend Cuba against American aggression. Kennedy publicly replied the United States would not permit the Soviet Union to establish a satellite in the Western Hemisphere or to endanger the nation's security by exporting communism to the rest of Latin America.*"

Textbook D, after summarizing the Bay of Pigs, simply notes: "*Castro, in turn, established even closer relationships with the Soviet Union.*"

With respect to the missile crisis, textbook F has a brief factual summary without analysis or comment, concluding: "*The Soviet Union backed down and Soviet ships bringing missiles to Cuba turned around and returned to Russia. Kennedy then lifted the blockade around Cuba."* Comment or supplementary information is, however, contained in most of the other texts.

Textbook A notes that *"there was an agonizing pause of five days before it was known whether Khrushchev would retreat from the brink of war. During this period the President was rewarded for his earlier restraint. The Organization of American States supported the United States by a vote of 19–0."*

Textbook B says nothing particularly noteworthy.

Textbook C is the only one to make clear that the U.S.S.R., using an American newspaperman to test out the idea, offered to withdraw the missiles under a three-point plan, and that this was accepted. First, the missiles would be dismantled and shipped back to the Soviet Union under U.N. supervision. Second, Castro would pledge himself to accept no offensive weapons in the future. Third, the United States would pledge itself not to invade Cuba.

Textbook C then comments: *"The conciliatory settlement of the Cuban missile crisis masked what was potentially the most dangerous confrontation in the Cold War. It not only averted war, but preserved a balance of power acceptable to both sides. American security in the Western Hemisphere was restored, while the Soviet Union gained assurance Cuba would not be subject to invasion. However, the continued presence of a revolutionary Communist state in the Western Hemisphere served to challenge the nation's traditional dominance in the Caribbean. . . ."*

Textbook D offers a summarization without comment—but also three readings that are supposed to illuminate the sequence of events. Those readings illustrate the difficulty of selecting the right materials for the "inquiry" approach.

Textbook D inadvertently distorts the correspondence between Kennedy and Khrushchev during the missile crisis because it has the wrong Khrushchev message. It offers, first, President Kennedy's television address to the nation in which he revealed the presence of the missiles in Cuba, warned the Soviet Union, and announced the quarantine. This was actually followed by a Khrushchev message that is not reproduced in textbook D, and by perhaps the most interesting link in the chain of communications, the use of ABC correspondent John Scali to inquire whether the United States would settle on the basis of the three-point program mentioned above (in connection with the treatment in textbook C). Neither the first Khrushchev message nor the proposal made through Scali is mentioned by textbook D.

Before Kennedy could reply to the Soviet proposal, another and much less conciliatory message from Khrushchev arrived. It is that message which textbook D reproduces in its entirety. (It contained a proposal that the United States dismantle its missiles in Turkey, something that columnist Walter Lippmann had thrown into the debate and that was considered unacceptable for a number of reasons.) What actually happened is that President Kennedy decided to ignore the second Khrushchev message and to accept the earlier three-point proposal. (Meanwhile John Scali was sent to meet his Soviet Embassy contact, whom he accused of a "stinking double-cross": Scali warned him that it was either the deal originally proposed by the U.S.S.R. or no deal at all.) Textbook D gives the impression that Kennedy's message of October 27, 1961, was in reply to the Khrushchev message of the same day. When events are complicated, selected documentary readings are usually not sufficient to explain what happened.

Textbook E devotes over fifteen pages to the Cuban Missile Crisis, but it has a similar difficulty. Among the readings is the appeal to President Kennedy and Chairman Khrushchev from U Thant, then the secretary-general of the United Nations. Because it called on both parties to stand back from the confrontation—the United States by suspending the quarantine, the U.S.S.R. by suspending further arms shipments—the appeal had a superficial plausibility. However, it played no role at all in the settlement, for reasons that are not explained. One is that a delay would have favored the Russians because it would have allowed the missiles already in Cuba to become operational. Also, U Thant's credentials in Washington had been tarnished by strong doubts about his impartiality on East-West issues. Washington considered that any hope of bringing about a withdrawal of the missiles from Cuba rested on a combination of firmness and restraint. Instead of explaining such complexities, textbook E merely introduces the U Thant letter with the comment that *"the United Nations did what it could to encourage efforts at negotiation and compromise."*

13
Early U.S. Involvement in Vietnam

Criteria

Was the war in Vietnam an anti-colonial liberation struggle, a civil war, or a war of aggression? Or was it all these things? Historians are not in agreement on all details, but most of them would probably agree that at least the early part of the war, which saw the Vietminh pitted against the French, had an anti-colonial character. That the French were recipients of American equipment and supplies is relevant. (This point has been discussed in another connection in section 10 above.) The treatment of the South Vietnamese regime that established itself after the Geneva Agreement of 1954 is more difficult. That regime was not subservient to the French, whom it ejected. It was not yet a creature of the Americans. It refused to sign the Geneva Agreement, suspecting the French of being so eager to get out of Indochina that they wouldn't mind consigning South Vietnam to the Communists. A relevant fact in that early history is that the United States, too, did not sign the Geneva Agreement.

Historians are also generally agreed that Ngo Dinh Diem, the first president of South Vietnam, was not popular, but there is disagreement whether that fact necessarily implies that the Communists were more popular. President Eisenhower said that if there had been elections in Vietnam in 1954, the Communists would have won them. However, the Geneva Agreement specified elections not in 1954 but in 1956, and by that time more than a million refugees had come to South Vietnam, bringing tales of the severities of the regime in the North. One plausible description of the early situation is that the South Vietnamese, while in the majority anti-Communist, were divided into so many factions and sects and cliques that democratic government was exceedingly difficult. Diem had a very bad press in the United States, and most Americans probably thought of him as a ruthless dictator. However, he cannot possibly have been an efficient dictator; for the very reason that South Vietnam was not as dictatorially ruled as North Vietnam, it experienced continuous squabbling among its politicians and later also among its generals.

Labeling the protagonists is a difficult matter, but Ho Chi Minh, the leader of the Vietminh and later of North Vietnam, was clearly a dedicated Communist. He had no use for non-Communist nationalists, whom he ruthlessly betrayed to the French. Nor did Diem claim to be a democrat. There is still some disagreement among historians whether the National Liberation Front, set up in 1960, was a Communist organization or a Communist-dominated coalition. There is agreement that it was supported (actually there is documentary evidence that it was controlled) by North Vietnam, but there are historians of the left who believe it had an independent existence. Because the subject is still contentious, it is difficult to establish criteria for fairness. It would not be too much to ask, however, that certain important facts, such as that Diem was not bound by the Geneva Agreement, should not go unmentioned.

Treatment

How do our textbooks manage this complex and controversial material? Textbooks C, D, and F do not mention that Ho Chi Minh was a Communist. Textbooks D and F imply that Ngo Dinh Diem broke the Geneva Agreement. Only textbook C mentions that South Vietnam had not signed it. All six textbooks mention that Diem's regime became increasingly unpopular. Most extraordinary, however, is the way some of them describe the National Liberation Front. Let us pass in review what they say.

Textbooks A and B are clearest about the Communist nature of the Vietminh. "*To complicate matters further*," says textbook A, "*the strongest leader of the Vietnamese independence movement, Ho Chi Minh, was a dedicated Communist, trained in Russia and China*." Textbook B says: "*The Vietminh (VYET-meen), a Communist group, had been fighting to win control of the entire country from the French and their anti-Communist Vietnamese allies. . . . During the late 1950's and early 1960's guerrillas known as the Vietcong, supported by Communist North Vietnam, ranged over the entire countryside of South Vietnam*."

Textbook A also states that after the French pulled out "*the United States moved into the vacuum and supported a rather shaky regime headed by an anti-Communist Vietnamese, Ngo Dinh Diem. American economic support enabled Diem to survive and to embark on some land reforms to aid the peasants. Increasingly, too, American 'advisers' and 'instructors' trained Diem's army*." On the relative unpopularity of the Diem regime, textbook A says: "*The governments of these [Indochinese] countries did not attract strong popular support and there was a constant threat of rebellion and infiltration by Communist guerrillas, who often terrified villages into submission.*" (Textbooks A and B are the only ones to mention terror tactics in connection with the Vietcong.) Later it says: "*Meanwhile, in spite of urgent advice from American officials to reform his regime, Diem's government became increasingly corrupt, repressive, and unpopular. Finally, in November 1963, Diem was overthrown and assassinated in a coup led by South Vietnamese officers. American officials had foreknowledge of the plot and had approved it. More than ever, the United States had assumed responsibility for whatever non-Communist regime attempted to rule in South Vietnam.*"

Textbook B says about Diem: "*By the spring of 1961 the struggle was going badly for the anti-communist government of President Ngo Dinh Diem (NOH DIN ZIM) whose repressive policies had antagonized many of his own people. . . . American efforts were frustrated . . . by the refusal of many South Vietnamese to support President Diem's unpopular government. Finally, in the fall of 1963, Diem was assassinated and his government was overthrown.*" Textbook B does not say how and by whom the National Liberation Front was organized, but it refers to "*organized terrorism and guerrilla warfare*" by the Vietcong, involving "*bombs planted in a country marketplace or in a busy city and the torture or assassination of unfriendly village leaders.*"

Textbook C speaks of "*communist-led Vietminh nationalists.*" About the Geneva Agreement it says that "*although the accords brought an end to the Indochinese war, the failure of all parties to accept them fully sowed the seeds of future conflict.*" This doesn't make clear that the South Vietnamese had not signed. Yet textbook C says: "*Elections were scheduled* [*by the Geneva agreement*] *for 1956, but these were later prevented by South Vietnamese premier Ngo Dinh Diem (an American-backed anti-Communist who succeeded Bao Dai in 1955) on the ground that existing conditions within Vietnam precluded a free choice.*" With respect to the Vietcong, it says: "*Opposition to Diem's repressive regime came from Buddhists, nationalists, and Communists who had joined together to form the National Liberation Front. . . .*"

Textbook D first says: "*In 1946, war broke out between the French and the Vietnamese nationalists. It lasted until 1954 when agreements were signed at Geneva ending the war. The agreements, known as the Geneva accords, divided Vietnam into two zones. The northern zone was placed under the government of the Vietminh league. The southern zone was placed under the control of the French army and a provisional South Vietnamese government. The French agreed to withdraw their troops when asked to do so by the government of the southern zone. The Geneva accords also stated that elections to decide the future government of Vietnam were to take place in 1956.*" Again, no mention that South Vietnam had not signed those accords.

Now come perhaps the two most interesting paragraphs. They are interesting for two reasons. First, they manage to overlook the fact that the Communists had something to do with the Vietminh, the NLF, and the Vietcong. Second, the first of the two paragraphs is identical in textbooks D and F, and the second virtually identical. (Questioned about this coincidence, the principal author of textbook D speculated that it might be the result of the publisher's "editing"; D and F have the same publisher.)

"*In 1955,*" say textbooks D and F, "*Ngo Dinh Diem, the French-educated leader of the southern zone, proclaimed a republic. He became its first president. He ignored the part of the Geneva accords which called for elections in 1956. He imposed a dictatorship on the republic of South Vietnam. He declared that this action was necessary because free elections could not be held in North Vietnam. Actually, Diem and the other South Vietnamese politicians feared that Ho Chi Minh, the popular nationalist leader, would win if any elections were held. Diem's actions were backed by the United States. The French army withdrew in 1956. By 1958, civil war had erupted in Vietnam.*" (It will have been noted that Ho Chi Minh is only a "popular nationalist leader.")

"*The United States had been training the South Vietnamese army since 1956,*" textbook D continues. "*When civil war broke out, it supplied military aid to Diem's forces. These forces were opposed in the south by the National Liberation Front. The NLF was a group of Vietnamese nationalists and pro-communists, supported by the government of North Vietnam. The military wing of this group was known as the Vietcong.*" Textbook F's version differs only in that it says: "*In South Vietnam, nationalists and pro-communists had formed the National Liberation Front (NLF) under the encouragement of Ho Chi*

Minh." Neither book even acknowledges that some Communists might have been among the NLF and the Vietcong. The coincidence between textbooks D and F continues. Both say that "*. . . the campaign begun by the NLF . . . won support from the peasants who made up the majority of the population*," and of course neither book mentions the assassinations, kidnappings, hostage-taking, blowing up of buses, throwing of bombs into marketplaces, and other terror tactics that were the staples of the Vietcong's plan to obtain control of the rural population. Yet there is no doubt that a portion of the rural population did voluntarily support the Vietcong. (Textbooks D and F correctly report the overthrow and killing of Diem in 1963.)

Textbook E treats the early years of the Vietnam War retrospectively, at the beginning of a collection of readings titled "The Decision to Risk a Compromise Peace in Vietnam." It says: "*There was a strong Communist movement in Indochina which had won its struggle against French colonial rule and caused the French to withdraw from Indochina in 1954. After the withdrawal of the French, the most highly developed part of Indochina—Vietnam—was divided into two parts. The Northern portion was controlled by a communist government under the leadership of Ho Chi Minh; the southern portion was controlled by a strong anti-communist government*." Textbook E has little to say about Diem, but it refers to the creation of the NLF as follows: "*Under President Kennedy . . . the amount of military equipment sent to South Vietnam was rapidly increased because of the outbreak of widespread guerrilla operations against the government by the Communist-supported National Liberation Front*." Again the impression is created that the NLF was a non-Communist organization only "supported" by the Communists. But even the Communists themselves did not claim that there were no Communists in the NLF! (They did, however, make use of non-Communist figureheads who never expressed any views other than those of the Communists.)

One can be of the opinion that Ho Chi Minh, the National Liberation Front, and the Vietcong were fighting a righteous cause and deserved to win. But that they were Communist or completely Communist-controlled is not a matter of opinion. The use of euphemistic phrases ("pro-Communist," "Communist-supported," "Communist-led," "nationalists and pro-Communists") seems to reflect reluctance to face a certain fact. Yet it is quite possible to be a Communist and a nationalist at the same time. We know this since Tito broke with Stalin in 1948, so it is hard to see why textbooks D and F, and to some extent textbook E, go through such contortions to elide the term *Communist* in connection with the war in South Vietnam. It is also noteworthy that while all the textbooks describe Diem's regime as "repressive," not one of them considers it necessary to make any similar remark about the regime in North Vietnam, which, being totalitarian, was far more repressive.

14
The Tonkin Gulf Resolution (1964)

Criteria

The controversial aspect of this material derives from the fact that when President Johnson asked Congress for a resolution in connection with the attack on American naval vessels in the Gulf of Tonkin, not all the facts surrounding that incident were revealed. Passed on August 7, 1964, the resolution authorized the President to "take all necessary steps, including the use of armed force," to assist certain Southeast Asian countries. It later turned out that Congress had been misled because the attacks against American warships had not been unprovoked: at about the same time there had been amphibious operations by the South Vietnamese with U.S. support against targets along the North Vietnamese coast. An adequate treatment would explain how the manner in which the Tonkin Gulf Resolution was obtained became one important factor when Congress later set stringent limits and eventually terminated all American support for the defense of South Vietnam.

Treatment

Only three textbooks deal with this important event. Textbook A writes: "*By summer of 1964 the Johnson regime moved toward the third alternative* [*of actively entering the war and attacking North Vietnam*]. *In secrecy the United States began limited bombing of the North and supported South Vietnamese commando raids on the North Vietnamese coast. In reprisal for one of the latter, North Vietnamese torpedo boats unsuccessfully attacked two American destroyers in the Tonkin Gulf. President Johnson then went to Congress and asked au-*

thorization to bomb the North. Thinking that the attacks on American warships had been unprovoked, Congress responded with the Tonkin Gulf Resolution. . . [which] authorized the President 'to take all necessary steps, including the use of armed force,' to protect any state in Southeast Asia. In effect, Congress abdicated its war powers to the President."

Textbook B is a bit less forthright, or at any rate less complete. It says only: "*In spite of some uncertainty about what had happened, the President announced on August 4, 1964, that two American destroyers had been attacked in the Gulf of Tonkin by North Vietnamese patrol torpedo boats and that he had immediately ordered retaliatory attacks. Three days later Congress adopted what became known as the Gulf of Tonkin Resolution. This resolution gave the President power to 'take all necessary measures to repel any armed attack against the forces of the United States and to prevent further aggression.*' "

To speak of "some uncertainty about what happened" is correct, but it provides only part of the truth. However, textbook B supplements the information a few pages later in connection with the Congressional hearings on Vietnam in 1968: "[*Secretary of State*] *Rusk reminded the* [*Foreign Affairs*] *committee that in the Gulf of Tonkin Resolution in 1964 Congress had authorized President Johnson to 'take all necessary measures to repel any armed attack against the forces of the United States and to prevent further aggression.' Senator Fulbright replied that when he voted for the resolution, he had not intended to give the President a 'blank check' to commit American troops to a land war in Asia.*" Actually, Senator Fulbright said a great deal more on that occasion. He said that if he had had the true facts, he would have voted against the Tonkin Gulf Resolution.

Textbook C contains more details about the attacks and the retaliatory steps taken, and it gives the salient passage of the resolution; but it notes only that the subsequent bombing of North Vietnam "*marked a significant departure from the 'advisory' role of Americans.*" It then comments on the further course of events: "*After the Tonkin Gulf incident, each new Vietcong attack was met by an escalation of the American military commitment. At the same time North Vietnam increased its infiltration of troops into South Vietnam. . . .* " But it gives no indication that the North Vietnamese action that triggered the Tonkin Gulf Resolution might not have been unprovoked.

Textbook D does not include the Tonkin Gulf incident and resolution in its summary or in its readings. Neither does textbook E. Textbook F, which devotes fifteen and a half pages to Vietnam as a "case study," has nothing on this turning point in the American involvement in the war and in the relationship between the Executive and Congress, a development that was to be fateful for the outcome of the war.

15
Late Vietnam Developments

Criteria

One can be a "hawk" or a "dove" about the last phase of the Vietnam War, but both hawks and doves agree that the Tet (Lunar New Year) offensive of February/March 1968 represented a turning point in American attitudes, both public and governmental, toward the war. After that offensive President Johnson removed himself from the 1968 presidential race and made renewed overtures to North Vietnam that resulted in the start of negotiations (of a sort) later that year. There was a clear shift in American public opinion in favor of a negotiated settlement, and anti-war activism on the campuses increased significantly. In retrospect, the sequence of events seems inexorable: a negotiated settlement involving American withdrawal, followed by a breakdown of the armistice, and eventually the collapse of South Vietnam. How can there be contention about those facts?

There is another side to almost all the foregoing statements. Although the Tet offensive was indeed a watershed event, it is now gradually coming to be recognized as a Communist military defeat, misreported and misinterpreted by the American mass media, which had been made skeptical by earlier over-optimistic government statements. Despite the political importance of campus unrest, according to public-opinion research a majority of young Americans (eighteen to twenty-nine years), more than any other age group, favored continuing support for South Vietnam as long as five years after the Tet offensive. Adequate treatment does not have to deal with such matters, but it should at least not give the misleading impression that the Tet offensive showed that the people in the Vietnamese towns and cities were on the side of the Communists, and it might point out that in the years immediately after that offensive, the government of South Vietnam vastly increased its control of the countryside because the South Vietnamese Communists (Vietcong) had virtually ceased to be a factor there.

Treatment

Here the publication dates of the six books are important. They are: A, 1973; B, 1977; C, 1975; D, 1975; E, 1975; and F, 1974. (Many of them are of course updates of earlier editions.) Therefore not all of them include the dénouement—or rather, the debacle—in Vietnam, but all appeared in time to note that the Tet offensive of 1968 represented a turning point in American involvement in the war.

Textbook A was apparently not revised to take all post-Tet developments into account. It says, "*The American military had grossly underestimated the will and ability of the Viet Cong to continue fighting, so the United States poured more and more troops into Vietnam and casualty lists mounted. . . .*" It describes domestic opposition to the war, noting that "*many clergymen of all faiths joined the 'doves', as those who favored termination of hostilities were called*" and referring to some of the prominent doves. Then it says: "*Opposed to the doves were the 'hawks', who supported the war. At least until the Tet offensive of 1968, public opinion polls revealed that they represented the dominant opinion among the American people and they were a majority in Congress.*"

Textbook B has three paragraphs on the Tet offensive as a turning point: "*Events in early 1968 demonstrated that Vietnamese doubts and fears were justified. Early in February the Vietcong and North Vietnamese army regulars opened the powerful Tet offensive—so-called because it was carried out during the Tet, or lunar New Year holidays. In a coordinated campaign they attacked the 'secure' cities of South Vietnam, seizing partial control of or terrorizing 25 provincial capitals.*

"*The South Vietnamese and American troops soon regained control of the capitals. But the price of 'victory' came high, for in the course of battle large sections of several cities were blasted into rubble. Equally serious, the Vietcong recovered control of large areas of the countryside.*

"*The Tet offensive dealt a staggering blow to an earlier prediction by General William Westmoreland, commander of America's military forces in South Vietnam, that the enemy was being defeated. It also demonstrated that the 'other war'—the effort of the Saigon government to win the allegiance of the Vietnamese people—was still far from won.*"

Textbook B then explains the Vietnamization policy, reports the changes in tactics ordered by President Nixon, refers to the so-called invasion of Cambodia in 1970, summarizes the Paris peace negotiations and the ceasefire agreement of 1973, tells how and why the war resumed after the departure of the Americans, and deals at some length with the trends in American opinion. Finally, it reports the Communist offensive of 1975, the refusal of Congress to supply any more aid, and the capture of Saigon. It then tells about the debate over the War Powers Act, by which Congress severely limited the President's authority to commit the United States to a war. It has no particular conclusion to offer about the end of the Vietnam War, except that "*with the Communist takeover . . . the tragic decades of fighting . . . came to an end.*"

Textbook C says: "*Vietcong strength was demonstrated early in 1968 during the Vietnamese New Year—Tet. Suddenly and explosively, Vietcong guerrillas launched a series of savage surprise attacks on major cities in South Vietnam. The Senate Foreign Relations Committee held hearings after the Tet offensive which resulted in a searching and critical analysis of American intervention.*" It then analyzes the points of view of both sides, and it describes the role that the war played in the presidential elections of 1968, the policy of Vietnamization, the crossing into Cambodia, the gradual withdrawal of American troops, and the armistice agreement of 1973. It notes that there was little celebration of the (presumed) end of "*a war that produced no famous victories, no national heroes, and no stirring patriotic songs,*" and ends by enumerating the costs—and predicting that conflict in Southeast Asia would probably continue.

Textbook D doesn't mention the Tet offensive. It also has no readings on that subject. It summarizes developments between 1955 and 1975 in this paragraph: "*The Vietnam war gradually became unpopular in the United States. Largely because of this development, President Lyndon B. Johnson decided not to run for re-election in 1968. His successor, Richard Nixon, promised to 'Vietnamize' the war. He said that he would withdraw American troops and train the South Vietnamese to fight their own war under the protective cover of American weapons. From 1969 until a cease fire agreement was reached in*

January 1973, American troops and casualties in Vietnam steadily declined. Organized opposition to the war also declined. However, a wave of violent demonstrations on many college campuses followed Nixon's decision to broaden the war temporarily by sending troops into Cambodia in the spring of 1971 [*sic*]." It then comments that "*the winding down of the Vietnam war seemed to mark a decisive change in the Cold War*," seeing this connected with the Nixon visits to Peking and Moscow and the policy of détente.

Textbook E devotes some fourteen pages to the Vietnam War, but the brief narrative portion merely says that "*after a surprise offensive launched by the Communists on January 29, 1968, had caused heavy American casualties, President Johnson decided to seek a negotiated settlement with North Vietnam.*" This is wrong on two counts: American casualties during the Tet offensive were not particularly heavy (the public-opinion response to that event was not primarily due to American casualties); and President Johnson had repeatedly sought a negotiated settlement with North Vietnam but the latter had refused to negotiate unless certain unacceptable preconditions were met. The basic change in position on negotiations came from the North Vietnamese, not from the American side. Textbook E then summarizes the Vietnamization policy, increasing opposition to the war in the United States, and the armistice agreement.

The readings of textbook E consist of pictures, poems, excerpts from speeches (for instance, Nixon's "Peace with Honor" announcement), and various commentaries. One of the questions put to the reader at the end of the Cold War chapter is, "*What role and how significant was the role played by the United Nations in each situation? How would you describe the UN's role over the course of these 25 years?*" However, since the student is not told that, for instance, the United States tried unsuccessfully many times to raise the subject of Vietnam in the United Nations (North Vietnam each time rejected "U.N. interference in Vietnamese affairs"), how is he supposed to be able to answer such a question?

We noted earlier that textbook F devotes twelve of the twenty-eight pages in its chapter entitled "The Cold War: Interpreting an Era" to Senator Joseph McCarthy. Perhaps because it regards the Cold War to have ended, the book contains another twenty-page chapter, "Facing the Future Abroad," which begins in about 1960 and contains a subchapter of fifteen and a half pages entitled "Vietnam: A Case Study," offering both narrative and readings. The Tet offensive is not mentioned, but there is a wealth of other material. There is, for instance, President Johnson's message to Ho Chi Minh of February 8, 1967, which, since it tried to induce negotiations without preconditions, avoided contentiousness as much as possible. It is compressed into half a page. Then a page and a half is devoted to Ho Chi Minh's February 15 reply to President Johnson, in which he rejected negotiation without preconditions but really addressed the world and the American public to propagandize his position: "Vietnam is thousands of miles from the United States. The Vietnamese people have never done any harm to the United States, but . . . the United States government has constantly intervened in Vietnam, has launched and intensified its aggression against South Vietnam for the purpose of prolonging the division of Vietnam and making South Vietnam into an American colony and an American military base. . . . The U.S. Government has committed war crimes against peace and against humanity. . . ."

Then there is Nixon's eight-point proposal, the North Vietnamese reply, a summary of the 1973 ceasefire agreement, and an item entitled "Vietnam: Pro and Con," in which four opponents of the war (John Knight, Senator Frank Church, D. F. Fleming, and Hans J. Morgenthau) give their views, while on the pro side only three paragraphs are allowed—and they do not seem to be selected for their effectiveness—to Secretary of State Dean Rusk. This is followed by a discussion of the Pentagon Papers, featuring a television interview between Walter Cronkite and Daniel Ellsberg, the former Department of Defense official who leaked the Pentagon Papers to the *New York Times*; Ellsberg concludes as follows: "There's never been . . . a [time during the past 25 years] when there [wasn't] war in Indochina with American money fueling it . . . and to say that is to say that Americans now bear major responsibility, as I read this history, for every death in combat in Indochina in the last 25 years, and that's one million to two million people." There is an item entitled "Reaction to the Release of the Papers," and the subchapter terminates with an article by Leslie H. Gelb that includes this passage: "The lesson of Vietnam should be no direct U.S. military intervention abroad except against [open] aggression by another great power and then only with the explicit approval of Congress." This would of course rule out not only another Vietnam but also U.S. help in another Korean War or intervention in a situation analogous to the Cuban Missile Crisis.

On the whole, the six textbooks convey the correct impression that the war in Vietnam ended the way it did because of increasing American war-weariness and disgust at its cost in human suffering, and that the Tet offensive played a major role in creating the impression that the war could not be won—and that even if it could, the game would not be worth the candle.

16
Has the Cold War Ended?

Criteria

No one knows whether the Cold War is over, but it is clear that Western relations with the Soviet Union and China are less strained today than they were, say, ten years ago. A high school textbook can thus legitimately give its reader the impression that the Cold War is a thing of the past, or it can suggest that because its basic causes have not been removed, the Cold War has only been muted but has not disappeared. One thing, however, is certain: "détente," defined as a relaxation of tensions, does not necessarily signify an end to the Cold War; nor does the fact that the United States and the Soviet Union have negotiated and are negotiating agreements on such matters as strategic arms limitation, in an effort to lessen the danger of a hot war.

One can take the position that the Cuban Missile Crisis, when the Soviets backed down, coming after the Soviet invasion of Hungary (and followed by that of Czechoslovakia), when the United States did not intervene, denoted that *de facto* spheres of influence were being recognized and that this signified the end of the Cold War. Or one can take the view that Communist power will continue to flow into any vacuum, that a stable "balance of terror" is required to preserve us from another world war, and that Vietnam, Angola, Ethiopia, and other recent events show that the U.S.S.R. and other Communist powers will seize every opportunity to extend the area under Communist domination.

Treatment

Textbook A, not surprisingly, considers that the Cold War is still going on today (though it has been "transmuted"). Textbook B, when it ascribes to President Nixon the view that "world conditions. . . had changed in many ways since the years of the Cold War," implies that it is over. So does Textbook C, which says that ". . . *the decade of the 1960's can be viewed as the dissipation of the Cold War—noted by the emergence of the third world and the passing of bipolarism*." Textbook D says that "*as the 70's moved toward their halfway mark . . . for the first time in more than a quarter of a century* [*Americans*] *were beginning to speculate about a possible end to the Cold War*." Textbook E says nothing on this aspect. Textbook F implies that it may be over, since it "continued through the 50's" and then presumably just petered out. The chapter of Textbook F that is entitled "The Cold War: Interpreting an Era" ends with the advent of the Kennedy Administration. The reader cannot be certain, however, whether textbook F really wishes to convey the point of view that the Cold War is over.

In any case, we must all hope that those who assert that the Cold War is over will be proved right.

THREE

Concluding Observations

The purpose of our analysis was not to "grade" the various textbooks. We have therefore resisted the temptation to tabulate whether and how they deal with the sixteen subjects, for this would have disadvantaged the "inquiry approach" textbooks, which tend to devote more pages to fewer subjects. Also, the awarding of "grades" to textbooks would inevitably involve too many subjective judgments.

Moreover, as indicated in chapter 1, high school history textbooks cannot be expected to be "complete." It is their very nature to cover only some aspects of a given period or subject. Textbook writers and their editors rightly concern themselves with making their books lively and interesting. It would be a disservice to judge them pedantically according to how thoroughly they cover a subject.

But when they leave out essential facts, when they do not present a coherent whole, or when they skew the evidence in one direction by their selection of readings or by a one-sided commentary on the body of facts, then an honest analysis should call attention to such situations.

Accuracy

On the whole, we do not find inaccuracy to be a major problem of these textbooks. That there should be some howlers is entirely understandable, for the writers of history textbooks cannot be experts on all the periods they cover. Thus one should not complain too much that one textbook speaks of Winston Churchill's speech at "Clayton, Missouri," or that another confuses two messages from Nikita Khrushchev to John Kennedy during the Cuban Missile Crisis.

Inaccuracies consist mainly of the omission of significant aspects of a particular event or situation. For instance, while several textbooks bring out *internal* American criticism of the Yalta Agreements in the late forties and early fifties, they slight the *international* controversy in

1945–47 over implementation of the Yalta Agreements between the United States and Great Britain on the one hand and the Soviet Union on the other.

However, slighting one aspect of the Yalta Agreements is one thing, and failing to mention the agreements at all is quite another. Textbook E, which is silent on Yalta, also excised a clause from the "Truman Doctrine" speech that referred to breaches of the Yalta Agreements. This could hardly have been an accident, since the speech is quoted extensively. Textbook F, which mentions Yalta in connection with World War II, has nothing about the bearing of the agreements on the Cold War.

Textbook F also fails to mention the containment policy. It does contain references to the Truman Doctrine, but it describes that statement inaccurately as committing the United States to "intervene in democratic revolutions everywhere." This is the *opposite* of what President Truman said. In a text given in textbook F itself, Truman juxtaposed Communism and democracy, making it clear that the United States stood for the latter.

Problems also exist with respect to the hazy description of the Vietcong as being "pro-Communist" or "Communist-led" or as being "an alliance of nationalists, Buddhists and Communists," as if it were not made up predominantly of Communists and completely controlled by them. However, for some people, convincing proof of this became available only after the end of the Vietnam war, when the Communists themselves said so. In any case, the treatment of Vietnam cannot be an adequate litmus test for textbook accuracy, since that controversial war is still so recent.

Scope, Fairness, and Balance

With the exception of one paragraph in textbook A, none of the textbooks can be said to present an overly favorable view of U.S. foreign policy. On the contrary, there is a tendency of several to give the Soviet Union greater benefit of the doubt than is given to the United States. That tendency is most marked in textbook F.

Any inadequacy in scope or balance cannot be explained in terms of space limitations, for the textbook that gives the most space to the Cold War (textbook E, with seventy-one pages) is one of those with the most significant gaps and omissions; whereas textbook B, which has relatively few inadequacies, has the second-smallest number of pages devoted to the Cold War (thirty). Textbook F, which, as we have noted, has the greatest amount of systematic bias, has exactly the median number of pages devoted to the Cold War (forty-eight, about the same number as textbook A).

Only two of the textbooks (A and F) deal with the subject of Communism, one that need not be covered in a textbook on American history—though it probably should be taught in the high school curriculum. Of these two, one (textbook A) explains the appeal of Communism but has only one sentence about its reality; while the other in effect offers an apologia of Communism, giving only a minimum of information about its unfavorable aspects.

Russian perceptions of the West are better explained, by those textbooks that deal with the subject, than Western perceptions of a threat from the East. For instance, textbook C, which in other respects is fairly well balanced, explains the Russian position in favorable terms but describes only the tactical restraint used by the West in countering Communist expansionist tendencies and not how those expansionist tendencies caused dismay and fear in the West. Textbook B has a good balance between the perceptions that the two sides had of each other.

All textbooks cover the Korean War, but some fail to bring out essential facts, e.g., that the U.N. Security Council was able to act only because the Soviet representative happened to be temporarily absent when the vote was taken. The most inadequate treatment is that of textbook F, which gives the erroneous impression that there were two separate forces helping the South Koreans, one provided by the United Nations, the other by the United States. Textbook F also fails to explain why China entered the war on the side of North Korea.

Several textbooks systematically glamorize the United Nations. This is most noteworthy in textbook B, which conveys the erroneous impression that the United Nations stopped the fighting in Palestine in 1948; that it helped to solve the Berlin crisis in 1949; that it (rather than the United States) governed events in the defense of South Korea; and that it made the withdrawal of foreign troops from Lebanon and Jordan possible in 1958. Textbook E conveys the erroneous impression that resort to the United Nations was an available alternative to the containment policy—although it recognizes that the Soviet Union could prevent any enforcement action by its veto. The same textbook exaggerates the U.N. role in the Cuban Missile Crisis, and it asks rhetorically "how significant was the role of the United Nations?" in connection with the Vietnam War without telling its readers why the U.N., despite American efforts, was prevented from playing any role whatever.

Textbook F is the only one that doesn't say anything about the Communist takeovers in Eastern Europe after World War II.

As for the policy of containment, textbook E has a "debate" that presents four opponents of the doctrine and no proponent. Textbooks A and B give a minimum of explanation. Textbook C is the most balanced. And textbook F has nothing on the subject.

McCarthyism is condemned sternly by textbook A; condemned somewhat less sternly by textbook B; rather fairly assessed—as an altogether excessive reaction to a genuine security problem—by textbook C; not mentioned in textbooks D and E; and given overly copious and not particularly enlightening treatment in textbook F, which does not refer to security problems at all and makes it appear that the excesses of the senator from Wisconsin were typical of prevailing attitudes in America at that time.

On Fidel Castro, textbooks B and C are the only ones to bring out the authoritarian or totalitarian character of his regime, while textbooks E and F turn a blind eye toward human rights in Cuba and emphasize social and economic progress. Textbook F gives the erroneous impression that Castro distributed land to the farmers who had worked it; does not mention collectivization; and gives credit to Castro for "wiping out widespread hunger by rationing food" without explaining that the food shortage had been brought about by his collectivization policies.

In dealing with Vietnam, all the textbooks portray Ngo Dinh Diem as unpopular, but certain important facts—e.g., that South Vietnam did not sign the 1954 Geneva Agreement—are mostly not brought out. (Textbook C is the only one to mention that South Vietnam was not a party to the Geneva Agreement.) There is a peculiar reluctance of textbooks D, E, and F to describe the Communist role in the Vietminh and the Vietcong, and textbooks D and F even manage to tiptoe around the fact that Ho Chi Minh was a Communist. Textbooks A and B are the only ones to mention that terrorism was an important tactic of the Vietminh and Vietcong.

In general, where clearly differing interpretations exist, few of the textbooks give both (or all) of them. There is less partisanship in textbook C, followed by A and B, than in the others. Textbook F unabashedly tilts to its preferred position, as when it presents a "debate" about Vietnam in which four opponents are given three times as much space as the single proponent of American policy, who is permitted to put forward only weak and unconvincing arguments.

It is impossible to generalize about all six textbooks. But it is possible to point out that several of them fail to give a coherent picture of the Cold War, fail to explain the interrelationship of events, fail to show how Western perceptions and policies were created by actions of the Communist powers, and fail to make clear the defensive nature of American foreign policy in the post–World War II period.

The problem is not whether the textbooks approve or disapprove of American foreign policies. In a democracy, constructive diversity is essential. But the high school pupil studying the Cold War period should be enabled to understand why the world in which we live is such a dangerous place, and what has happened during the last three decades to make cooperation between East and West so difficult.

The Two Teaching Approaches

Textbooks A, B, and C are mainly narrative; textbooks D, E, and F consist mainly of readings, representing the "inquiry approach." We regard it as an accident that textbooks A, B, and C are generally in the center of the political spectrum whereas textbooks D, E, and F are generally to the left, ranging in some cases (notably F) to the extreme left. While it is natural that authors hold differing views, those who express their views through a one-sided selection of readings tend to introduce their point of view more surreptitiously. Often the phrasing of questions addressed to the student accentuates this shortcoming.

It seems to us after surveying the "inquiry approach" textbooks that this approach is peculiarly ill-suited to the teaching of a complicated chain of events such as the Cold War, which requires a coherent narrative to explain the interrelations between those events. At the very least, "inquiry" textbooks should include persuasive documents plausibly explaining the policies that the writers of the textbooks may not like. This they conspicuously fail to do.

The selected readings provided by textbooks D, E, and F do not deal with the origins and the nature of the Cold War; textbooks E and F have nothing on the disagreements over Yalta; textbook E has a seriously unbalanced "debate" about containment; textbook F, which misrepresents the Truman Doctrine, asks the student rhetorically whether a militant speech by President Truman "might have eased [the tensions of the Cold War] or made them worse" without giving anything about the historical setting of that speech; textbook E also exaggerates the capacity of the United Nations to deal with problems between the super-powers; textbook F, though it devotes twelve pages to Senator Joseph McCarthy, manages to overlook what may have been the most important reason for his influence; textbooks D, E, and F tilt toward Castro in their accounts of his rule; and textbooks E and F manage to blur and obfuscate—despite copious readings on the subject—the nature of the enemy we fought in Vietnam.

It is interesting, and possibly significant, that the textbook that contains the warning against bias cited in chapter 1 (it is textbook E) is among those that provide the readers with a rather unbalanced diet of documentary readings—for instance, in the selections on the containment policy.

Because it would be just as easy for writers of the opposite persuasion to assemble readings that tilt in the opposite direction, we conclude that the "inquiry approach" does not necessarily pose the danger of tilting in the direction of textbooks D, E, and F. It seems to us that this technique poses, quite generally, the danger of surreptitious direction of the minds of young people toward author-preferred conclusions and that such attempts to lead students would be more easily recognized in narrative textbooks. Why? Because while the "on the one hand, on the other hand" approach of a narrative treatment allows an author to set up a straw man and knock him down, this will be more apparent to the reader; whereas with the inquiry approach the reader might not notice, because of the seeming diversity of the material, that the selected readings were entirely on one side of an issue.

If it is true, as some proponents and opponents of the "inquiry approach" seem to agree, that this teaching method addresses itself especially to the brightest students with the highest reading ability, then the question arises whether the "best and the brightest" among our high school students may not, at least when it comes to their knowledge of recent history, be also the most one-sidedly informed—and at the same time the most confident that they have recognized and avoided bias in their study of our recent history.